Find Your Way

A Story and Drama Resource to Promote Mental Well-being in Young People

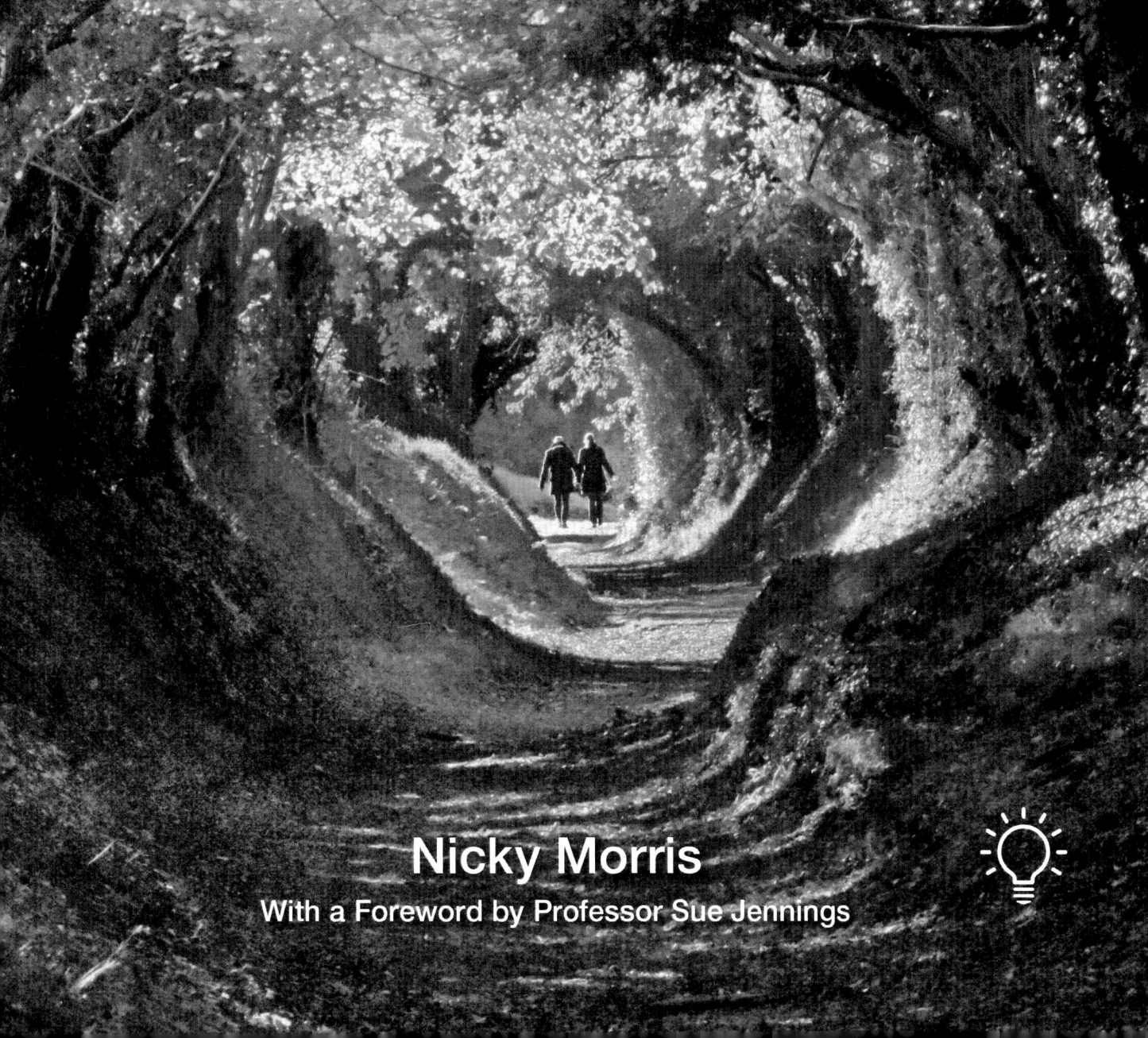

Nicky Morris

With a Foreword by Professor Sue Jennings

Find Your Way

© Nicky Morris

The author has asserted her rights in accordance with the Copyright, Designs and Patents Act (1988) to be identified as the authors of this work.

Published by:
Pavilion Publishing and Media Ltd
Blue Sky Offices
Cecil Pashley Way
Shoreham by Sea
West Sussex
BN43 5FF
UK

Tel: 01273 434 943

First published 2020

All rights reserved. No part of this publication may be reproduced, stored in a retrieval system, or transmitted in any form or by any means, electronic, mechanical, photocopying, recording or otherwise, without the prior permission in writing of the publisher and the copyright owners.

A catalogue record for this book is available from the British Library.

ISBN: 978-1-913414-11-5

Pavilion Publishing and Media is a leading publisher of books, training materials and digital content in mental health, social care and allied fields. Pavilion and its imprints offer must-have knowledge and innovative learning solutions underpinned by sound research and professional values.

Author: Nicky Morris
Editor: Ruth Chalmers, Pavilion Publishing and Media
Cover design: Phil Morash, Pavilion Publishing and Media
Page layout and typesetting: Phil Morash, Pavilion Publishing and Media
Printing: Ashford Press

'This is great. I really found this so enjoyable and easy to read/navigate, which is a good thing for a busy teacher. I feel that the layout and the scenarios are easy to connect with and easy to imagine implementing in any classroom. I can see this being a great go to resource for many teachers, to help navigate some of the challenging topics that exist in our school communities that can help them feel empowered and secure to deliver. This book also shows the importance and value of Drama being an important subject that enables a safe and vital place to explore these activities.'

Andria Zafirakou MBE. Global Teacher Prize Winner 2018. Consultant on Creativity and Innovation. Speaker. Art and Textiles Teacher. Founder and CEO of Artists in Residence (AiR) Charity.

'This book shows us the innate power of story. The carefully chosen stories and structures offered in Nicky Morris' book offer huge potential for them to be used in a variety of clinical, creative or educational settings. Not only are we introduced to a range of differing stories and the theoretical notions behind them, but a series of structured suggestions including, discussion, dramatic performance, art work, creative writing and improvisation. All of this is followed by examples of how Nicky has used the stories herself. This book offers both the novice and experienced therapist, artist or teacher a treasure trove of ideas which can be used at different levels and in different contexts for many years to come.'

Dr Clive Holmwood, Associate Professor, Department of Therapeutic Arts University of Derby.

'As a Dramatherapist of almost twenty-five years, stories are a staple part of my work and I am always on the look-out for new ones.

In her new book, Nicky Morris offers ten new stories and a unique structure of ways to work with them.

Young people are the future and yet are vulnerable as they struggle to emerge as adults in an ever changing society, with new stressors and challenges.

The stories that Nicky has written, offer opportunities to explore these challenges contained within metaphor and character, often animals, which allows for dramatic distancing and an oblique way to explore the trials of 21st century life. In addition, eternal and pervading issues such as identity, attachment and separation, companionship, moving on from trauma, loss, starting anew and integrating aspects of the self, are present within the narratives. The stories are beautifully written and illustrated.

In this book, Nicky explains the prevalence of struggle and mental health issues in adolescents and the power of story. She then expertly and in great detail demonstrates how to work with the stories. The guide includes exercises to lead into the stories, a script for each, how to work and respond with artwork and writing and with drama and improvisation.

Each story is incomplete so that the ending can be explored and found by the individual or group working with the story. This avoids offering a moral or direction that precludes choice. Instead, an experience of empowerment is offered through the client or pupil defining the ending.

The book also describes how the stories were created and vignettes of therapeutic and school-based sessions, where the stories have been used.

This book will be a unique resource for dramatherapists, teachers, students, individuals who would like to explore the stories independently and other health and education practitioners – and I cannot recommend it highly enough.'

Kate McCormack – Senior Dramatherapist in the NHS.

'It is a real pleasure to read, engage with, and learn from the therapeutic approach outlined in this book by Nicky Morris. Nicky highlights the therapeutic benefits of creating a 'psychological safe space', of being alongside the patient in experiencing their difficulties, and seeking a co-created way forward through development of a meaningful narrative that blends the patient's present, past and future truths – 'each finding their own way' in doing this. Nicky's contributions to the therapeutic work with these patients, brought to life in this book and in their treatments, incorporates and guides all the values of an effective Multi-Disciplinary Team working together with distressed, young people on their therapeutic, developmental journeys. Reading this book, reflecting on it, and making the approaches clearly outlined here, your own to use, is time well spent for all professionals and young people engaged in, and seeking to learn through, this intensive and rewarding therapeutic work.'

Dr Kevin Healy, Retired Consultant Psychiatrist, ex-chair of the Faculty of Medical Psychotherapy, Royal College of Psychiatrists, ex-chair Association of Therapeutic Communities.

Contents

Foreword 7

Introduction 9

Story 1: *The Glow Fish* 25
Attachment, separation and personality types

Story 2: *The Lost One* 39
Past, Future, Present

Story 3: *Guardian of Dogs* 53
Rejection, Abuse, Trust and Recovery

Story 4: *Boy in a Tree* 69
Avoidance, Self-Preservation, Fear and Courage

Story 5: *Little Blue* 83
Immigration, Expectations, Relationships and Prejudice

Story 6: *The Glass Wall* 97
Confinement and Freedom, Attachment and Separation

Story 7: *Silver Angel* 107
Friendship, Transformation and Loss

Story 8: *Born of Shadow and Light* 119
Emotional Balance

Story 9: *Survivors* 131
Inner Strength and Courage

Story 10: *Nature's Spirits* 143
Environmental Issues, Personality Types and Choice

Appendix 155

Foreword

I feel very privileged to be writing the foreword to this remarkable book, *Find Your Way: A Story and Drama Resource to Promote Well-being in Young People*.

There is a comprehensive introduction which reminds us that drama and stories are essential for mental well-being, in particular with young people, where suicide is the second cause of death amongst 15-29 year olds. The author draws our attention to the 'All Party Parliamentary Group on Arts, Health and Wellbeing' (APPGAHW) who say:

'Arts participation helps to overcome anxiety, depression and stress in parents and their children, encouraging bonding and emotional expression'.

It is a salutary reminder that half of all mental health conditions are thought to begin by the age of 14 and two thirds by 19 years. This illuminating book gives a very solid framework for creative activities with young people. These include young women with anxiety, depression, eating disorders, EUPD (emotional unstable personality disorders), psychotic disorders and more.

Following the introduction, the unique design of this book gives us ten sections, described as 'a pack', and you can see why. Each section has its own introduction, description of client group, selected themes, narrative, mini-script and suggestions for exploration including discussion, improvisation, creative writing, poetry, movement, voice work and craft work. The story, once told, is left incomplete for individuals and groups to explore, or decide on the possible ending. What is important is that a secure structure is given but with as much choice as possible.

The ten stories explore, through metaphor and some animal characters, themes of:

attachment, separation, rejection, abuse, neglect, abandonment, bereavement, loss, avoidance, self-preservation, relationships, communication, fear, courage, prejudice, betrayal, freedom, friendship and current global issues of the environment and pollution. Just these examples alone remind us what a complex range of emotions are around for vulnerable young people.

There are clear and detailed guidelines on how to apply these stories, and the necessary safeguards.

My favourite stories are in fact the first two. *The Glow Fish*, looking at attachment, separation and personality types, explores being able to move forward when you are stuck, the fear and freedom of moving on (or moving out), and much more. The second story, *The Lost One*, explores past, future and present. The central character is called Perdu and she remembers nothing apart from her name, suffering depression, anxiety, grief and dissociation. There are four doors, to the past, the future, the present and back to slumber. I practised this narrative on myself and found it very illuminating! I discovered that I followed the door to my past too readily and avoided the present! My appreciation to the author.

Story number 4, *The Boy in the Tree*, is an excellent resource for therapists, parents and teachers working with young people on the autistic spectrum.

Although this book has emerged from research and practice with young people, the stories and techniques can also be adapted for older children and adults. *The Guardian of Dogs*, story 3, for example, is a very flexible story and could be explored with children in the care system or looked after children. Story 7, *Silver Angel*, could be adapted for working with older people, as it addresses themes of loss, friendship and frustration.

This book is a remarkable resource from an experienced and knowledgeable professional. It integrates theory and practice for the application of drama and stories with vulnerable populations, backed up by the most recent knowledge. It is also a very enjoyable and accessible book to read.

Professor Sue Jennings
Wells and Kuala Lumpur
Senior Research Fellow, The Shakespeare Institute
University of Birmingham

Introduction

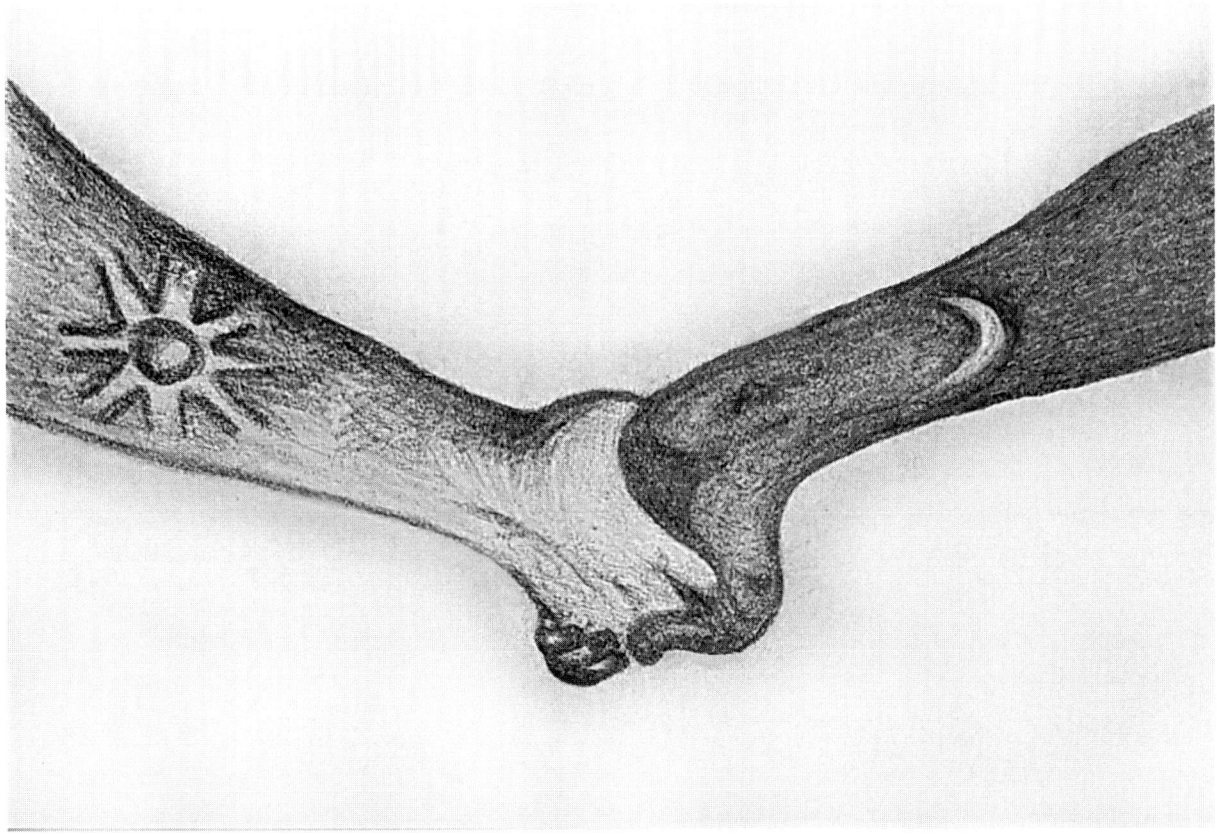

Illustration by Nicky Morris

Promoting mental well-being in young people

'The social challenge of our time is to reverse the growing level of mental ill health. Good mental health is fundamental to thriving in life. It is the essence of who we are and how we experience the world.' (Mental Health Foundation, 2020)

Mental health is a growing global concern and research from the World Health Organisation reveals that, tragically, suicide remains the second leading cause of death among 15–29 year olds (WHO, 2019). Promoting positive mental well-being in adolescents and young adults is therefore vital and innovative approaches are essential.

Relevant to readers across the globe, this pack offers a research and practice-based approach, designed to promote well-being in adolescents and young adults. It contains a collection of 10 original stories, accompanied by mini scripts and creative activities, which offer people a unique way in which to explore the challenges they face in the modern world. While some encourage reflective thinking, others are more solution-focused. However, suffused with metaphor, each one provides a safe platform from which to explore sensitive themes: isolation, trauma, abandonment, loss, mistreatment, relationships, independence, immigration, prejudice, hope and recovery. Choices are offered at the end of each story, allowing people to choose their own ending. This process is empowering and encourages self-determination. It can also provide facilitators with a creative tool through which to assess mood and mental state, while helping individuals to make sense of themselves and others.

Half of all mental health conditions are believed to begin by the age of 14 and two-thirds by the age of 19 (NHS, 2019, p50). In the UK, the National Health Service has identified the need to extend and improve its current mental health services to 0–25 year olds, with a focus on eliminating the gap that exists when young people transition into adult services. It explains that, 'Between the ages of 16 [and] 18, young people are more susceptible to mental illness, undergoing physiological change and making important transitions in their lives' (NHS, 2019, p51). The challenges that young people face in modern society are further complicated by the growing dominance of social media. The National Center for Health Research in the US has revealed that, while social media can have a positive impact on well-adjusted adolescents, it can be detrimental to the mental health of those who are more vulnerable or less popular (Mir and Novas, 2017). Similarly, for young adults aged 19–32, increased social media use has been linked to a rise of perceived social isolation (Primack *et al*, 2017) and an increase in depressive symptoms (Shensa *et al*, 2017). For young women, certain sites are also associated with increasing body-image concerns and self-objectification (Feltman and Szymanski, 2018, p6).

The UK government published a White Paper in 2019 titled *Online Harm*. While recognising the internet's potential to be a powerful force for good – enhancing freedom and opportunities across the globe – it highlights that 'harmful content and activity can be particularly damaging for children and young people, and there are growing concerns about the potential impact on their mental health and well-being' (HM Government, 2019, p11). Communicating via social media remains a significant (and necessary) aspect of modern life. It should be balanced, however, with face-to-face, positive interaction. This is where the arts can play a significant role and structured creative activities used to support the mental well-being of young people. As revealed in a detailed report from the UK's All-Party Parliamentary Group on Arts, Health and Well-being (APPGAHW), 'Arts participation helps to overcome anxiety, depression and stress in parents and their children, encouraging bonding and emotional expression' (2017a, p11).

How stories and creative activities can help

The stories, scripts and creative activities in this pack can be used with both groups and individuals. They may stimulate either reflective or active therapeutic work with adolescents and young adults challenged by a range of emotional and mental health difficulties. The themes that arise can be explored through discussion and/ or enactment, such as improvisation, group tableaus, script-work and character development, etc. Methods such as roleplay and hot-seating can be applied and projective techniques are also effective, allowing people to express their individual responses to chosen characters, specific moments, themes, etc. Working either spontaneously or with the scripts offered will help to improve confidence and develop communication skills. Expressive movement and facial and vocal expression are also encouraged, together with group collaboration, imaginative thinking and creativity. Finally, there is the potential for creative writing (as none of the stories have a definitive ending) as well as responses expressed through music, poetry, art and craft work.

Pertinent to people of different nationalities and cultures, the stories in this collection address relationships, self-esteem and self-actualisation, while incorporating world and political themes. Although the focus varies between each one, they all promote choice, independent thinking and decision making. Each one has a clear rationale, with key themes to explore, making them a valuable new resource for dramatherapists, drama and movement therapists, dance movement psychotherapists, integrative arts psychotherapists, hypnotherapists and trainees. Furthermore, they will prove useful for teachers, storytellers, psychotherapists, counsellors, mental health workers and students, as well as for any individual concerned with their own mental health and seeking ways to understand themselves further. Training workshops can also be arranged to support the work.

The stories, scripts and activities have been used in Dramatherapy sessions, with many young women, with a variety of diagnoses and difficulties: depression, anxiety, emotionally unstable personality disorder (EUPD), psychotic disorders (such as paranoid schizophrenia), eating disorders, post-traumatic stress disorder (PTSD) and autistic spectrum disorder (ASD). To demonstrate their potential, examples of clinical practice are shared in the 10 story chapters. Other examples are also given, such as how one story was used to support mental health colleagues in a team-building context and another presented to a group of professionals at a hypnotherapy conference, for which Darren Marks offers feedback. Finally, Dom Roy, an English teacher and Head of Year 11 at a boys' secondary school, reflects on how he and his students responded to two of the stories.

Drama and the arts for mental health

'The act of creation, and our appreciation of it, provides an individual experience that can have positive effects on our physical and mental health and well-being.' (APPGAHW, 2017a, p10)

The UK's All-Party Parliamentary Group on Arts, Health and Well-being (APPGAHW) formed in 2014, to carry out research into the benefits of the arts for health and well-being for people of all ages in different social settings, with a variety of needs. In 2017, it published its results and recommendations, hoping to improve policy and practice across the UK. It recognises that, 'The creative impulse is fundamental to the experience of being human' (APPGAHW, 2017a, p10). There are many forms through which we can express ourselves creatively, either individually or with others: they include drama, dance, film, music making, singing, art, craft, design, creative writing and the creative use of digital media.

The APPGAHW has identified the positive impact of engaging with the arts in eight areas:

1. Health and care environments (hospitals, GP surgeries, hospices and care homes etc.).
2. Participatory arts programmes (individual and group arts activities, established to improve and maintain health and well-being in health and social care settings and community locations).
3. Arts therapy sessions (usually in clinical settings – facilitated by Drama, Art and Music Therapists, professionals accredited by the HCPC).
4. Arts on prescription (part of social prescribing for people experiencing psychological or physical distress, encouraged to access the arts in the community, such as visiting galleries, museums and libraries etc.).
5. Medical training and medical humanities (including the arts in the professional development of health and social care professionals).
6. Everyday creativity (drawing, painting, pottery, sculpture, music or filmmaking, singing or handicrafts etc.).
7. Attendance of cultural venues and events (concert halls, galleries, heritage sites, libraries, museums and theatres etc.).
8. Built and natural environments (improving the environment in which people live, such as maintaining parks).

(2019, pp8–9)

The stories, scripts and activities in this pack could be used to support the creative work offered in five of the above areas: 1 (health and care environments), 2 (participatory arts programmes), 3 (arts therapy sessions), 5 (medical training and medical humanities) and 6 (everyday creativity).

The APPGAHW concludes that (2019, p4):

1. The arts can help keep us well, aid our recovery and support longer lives better lived.
2. The arts can help meet major challenges facing health and social care: ageing, long-term conditions, loneliness and mental health.
3. The arts can help save money in the health service and social care.

The APPGAHW recognises the importance of encouraging health and social care commissioners across the UK to consider the evidence they have compiled and apply it to key areas, such as the guidelines offered to clinicians by NICE (National Institute for Health and Care Excellence). During a meeting held between the APPGAHW and NICE, the Director of the Centre for Guidelines 'observed that the arts were conspicuous by their absence in guidelines on mental health and indicated that this might be rectified' (APPGAHW, 2019, p39).

Drama and the arts have been used throughout the world for centuries, providing opportunities for education and transformation. Using the arts to support both mental and physical well-being is therefore an ancient rather than a modern concept. Historically, the arts have been linked to healing and although their role may have decreased in many cultures with the rise of Western medicine, it was revived in the 20th century in the form of the arts therapies (Jones, 2007, p66). Dramatherapy, art therapy and music therapy began to appear as distinct professions in the 1940s and are now recognised in many countries as an integral part of health and care systems (Jones, 2007, p3). As the UK's APPGAHW states in its report, 'Arts therapies have been found to alleviate anxiety, depression and stress while increasing resilience and well-being' (2017a, p9).

Dramatherapy

Dramatherapy is a form of psychological therapy in which all of the performance arts are utilised within the therapeutic relationship. Dramatherapists are both artists and clinicians and draw on their training in theatre/drama and therapy to create methods to engage clients in effecting psychological, emotional and social changes (British Association of Dramatherapy, 2020).

Peter Slade was the first person to put the words drama and therapy together, publishing his pivotal paper *Dramatherapy as an aid to becoming a person* in 1959 (Jennings, 2016, XX). In the late 1960s and early 1970s, he then supported Marian (Billy) Lindkvist in her efforts to develop the Sesame approach of drama and movement therapy (Lindkvist, 2007 l.1536-1539) and also supported Sue Jennings in her quest to establish a professional association for dramatherapists (Jennings, 2007, l.1574-1576). With passion and perseverance, Jennings founded the British Association of Dramatherapy (BADth) in 1976 and continues to pioneer both Dramatherapy and Play Therapy across the World, establishing and contributing to many training programmes.

Inspired by the ancient world, Dramatherapy practice anchors itself in the modern world, allowing psychological and theatrical elements to unite. Theatre originated in ancient Greece, as a union of poetry, myth, dance, music, healing and religious rituals. In Greek tragedy, Aristotle identified the significance of catharsis, a process that allowed Athenian audiences to witness the tragic component of humanity in its purest form, helping them to understand and accept the limitations of being human (Levine, 2005, p56). Reconnecting to this earlier, more spiritual aspect of theatre, Mary Smail, an innovative dramatherapist of the 21st century, has developed a Psyche and Soma course for arts therapists (and other education and health professionals) through which they can explore the notion of 'soul' and its place within modern therapeutic practice (Smail, 2020). Her course draws upon key components of the Sesame approach, including Jung's concept of dreaming and the story-making unconscious, and Hillman's re-visioning of psychology through soul work (Hillman, 1997, XV). Rather than attempt to offer solid answers to fluid, existential questions, Smail offers initial findings and encourages more questions (2016, p187) which mirrors the approach I have taken with the stories offered in this book.

Bessel Van der Kolk, psychiatrist and author of the seminal work *The Body Keeps The Score*, describes several approaches to transforming the experience of trauma, using the mind, brain and body. In his research, Van der Kolk recognises the significance of ancient Greek theatre (communal drama, dance, music and ritual) in relation to modern theatre and its role in helping individuals and communities to heal from trauma (2015, pp331–346). He also shares how he experienced its potential on a personal level, after witnessing his son recover from a debilitating illness, by attending improvisational theatre classes (2015, p330). Focusing on theatre for trauma, Van der Kolk writes, '… there are many excellent therapeutic drama programs in the United States and abroad, making theatre a widely available resource for recovery. Despite their differences, all of these programs share a common foundation: confrontation of the painful realities of life and symbolic transformation through communal action.' (2015, p335)

Stories from across the world, both old and new, are a fundamental resource for dramatherapists. While traditional stories offer a rich variety of themes, new stories may also be written and familiar ones transformed. May suggests that myth making is crucial to improving mental health, offering people 'a way of making sense in a senseless world' (1991, p15).

Stories to promote mental well-being

'You can't live without stories, without telling them and making them. You yourself are a story: a story of how you have been and hope to be, of how you are and might be.' (Parkinson, 2009, p17)

Gersie, a renowned storyteller and dramatherapist, explains that stories bring life and form to the issues that are most pertinent to humankind, and that telling our stories is crucial to personal development: 'They help us both to grow up and to become more like ourselves. A generous capacity to tell and a warm capacity to listen support a comfortable fit between us and our world' (1997, l.42–43). Through a range of responses to the stories and activities offered in this collection, individuals are given the opportunity to express aspects of their own stories, both reflectively and creatively. This may be either conscious or unconscious, and relates to Jung's assertion that while clinical diagnoses are important, 'The crucial thing is the story. For it alone shows the human background and the human suffering, and only at that point can the doctor's therapy begin to operate' (Jung, 1993).

Many hypnotherapists use suggestive stories, scripts and therapeutic metaphors in their sessions, an approach influenced by the work of Erickson, a psychiatrist who treated medical conditions using hypnosis. Through stories, metaphors and parables, he taught his clients what they needed to know in order to make the changes they sought (Nongard and Hazlerig, 2014, l.1999). His approach contrasts entirely with stage hypnosis, an authoritarian style that relies on a mix of theatre and social compliance. The Ericksonian method instead encourages the hypnotist and client to work together, one changing the other, to allow a process of transformation (Nongard and Hazlerig, 2014, ll.135–155). Resonating deeply with people, stories and metaphors can tap into a person's unconscious and inspire positive change. As Nongard and Hazlerig explain, 'Erickson saw the unconscious mind as being infinitely intelligent, a reservoir of solutions and creativity' (2014, l.116).

Stories are an invaluable tool through which one can connect with people, especially those who may appreciate and respond more willingly to a less direct approach. They can then be used to promote mental well-being, by allowing people to explore significant issues and emotions, within the safety of aesthetic or dramatic distance. Jennings explains that in Dramatherapy, dramatic distancing 'provides a structure for participants that paradoxically brings them closer to themselves' (1990, p21). This is emphasised by Schrader, in her description of myth enactment with a ritual theatre group. She describes how individuals were able to fully express their suppressed anger, sadness, grief or rage, through playing dramatic characters – adding that only after the enactment 'the client becomes aware of what they have actually been working on and addressing in their own psyche and history' (Schrader, 2012, p185–186).

Through stories and story characters, individuals can express and process a range of emotions without having to name them directly. By using Lahad's 6-Part Story Method (6-PSM), for example, therapists can visualise a map of the inner world of their clients, then plan the most appropriate interventions for them. The 6-PSM is often used as a Dramatherapy assessment tool and the most current version includes seven levels of analysis for the therapist. Lahad explains: 'When I introduced the 6PSM as an assessment tool, my assumption was that by asking the client to tell a projected story based on elements of fairy tale and myth, we might be able to see the way that the self projects itself into reality in order to "meet" the world' (Lahad, 2013, p48).

Folk stories, fairy tales and myths encompass the Jungian concept of archetypes and the collective unconscious (Jung, 1968). As Campbell explains, 'All over the world and at different times of human history, these archetypes, or elementary ideas, have appeared in different costumes' (1991, p61). Working with them then encourages a deeper understanding and acceptance of self and others, which supports mental well-being. The HCPC (Health and Care Professions Council) defines Dramatherapy as 'a unique form of psychotherapy in which creativity, play, movement, voice, storytelling, dramatisation, improvisation and the performance arts have a central position within the therapeutic relationship' (2013). Stories (and story characters in particular) have always featured in my own work and several have been especially effective. Examples include *The First Sunrise* (an Aboriginal Dreamtime story), *The Brave Little Parrott* (an ancient Jataka tale from India), *The Wonderful Wizard of Oz* (Baum, 1900), *The Adventures of Alice in Wonderland* (Carroll, 1865) and *Winnie the Pooh* (Milne, 1926). New stories have also been created with clients. Themes are explored, characters chosen, tableaus formed and simple lines devised.

Introduction

Developing the stories in this collection

I began to write the stories in this collection to help me to connect with a group of complex female clients who were particularly withdrawn. The stories then opened up a new dialogue with these young women and it also became clear that they had the potential to relate to a variety of people: adolescents and adults, male and female, with a range of emotional and/or mental health difficulties. Animal characters are used in seven of the ten stories, adding a further layer of safety offered through metaphor. Furthermore, I discovered the appeal of the stories to other professionals working in health and education. I introduced *The Glow Fish* to a group of delegates at a hypnotherapy conference, for example, and later workshopped *Nature's Spirits* with a group of mental health colleagues at a team building day. As the APPGAHW reveals, 'Cultural engagement and arts therapy can improve well-being in healthcare staff' (2017b, p1). Dom Roy, an English teacher and Head of Year 11 at a boys' secondary school, then worked with *Boy in a Tree* and *Little Blue* with two groups of students. His reflections are shared in detail in the relevant story chapters.

I have worked as a dramatherapist in mental health services for more than 15 years and continue to explore new ways in which to support my clients. A pervasive feeling of hopelessness is often present, as the young people I work with have encountered extreme adversity in their lives. Many of them question their existence and remain ambivalent about life and death (Morris, 2018, p132). Finding meaning in one's life is essential, as without it individuals may feel worthless and life can appear senseless. While supporting my clients in their search for meaning, I remain aware of my own struggle with similar existential issues. As Yalom explains, while self-awareness makes us human, it also reveals our mortality: 'Our existence is forever shadowed by the knowledge that we will grow, blossom, and, inevitably, diminish and die' (2008, p1). As well as supporting clients, colleagues and students, I have learnt that it is crucial to take care of one's own mental and physical health. This enables one to genuinely support others and to manage the various challenges, dynamics and existential issues that may arise. If working in a clinical setting, this must also include regular supervision.

While developing the stories and scripts in this collection, I have received helpful feedback from a variety of sources: my two daughters, Lucy and Ella; my clinical supervisor, Kate McCormack; my colleague, Dr Preeti; Shelley Morris (Head of English at a girls' secondary school); and Dom Roy (Head of Year 11 and an English teacher at a boys' secondary school). Introducing the stories to clients then helped me to improve them further, and the creative activities that evolved are included in this pack. I also discovered that while some clients were keen to improvise in response to the stories, others felt more comfortable working with scripts. I then developed scripts to accompany the stories, or tableau sequences, with suggested text.

Having supported MA Dramatherapy students on clinical placements since 2006 (and facilitating teaching workshops on the MA Dramatherapy courses at both Roehampton University and Anglia Ruskin University, Cambridge), I have observed that trainees often struggle to apply what they are learning to their clinical practice and are keen to acquire specific creative tools. The stories, scripts and activities in this collection fulfil this need and should be easily applicable and relevant to Dramatherapy trainees, as well as those from other professions. They will also provide an extra resource to those who are already qualified.

A summary of the ten stories

Gersie suggests that traditional stories highlight the natural pull towards growth or maturation and that sooner or later, 'Every story character is invited to wake up and to grow up' (1997, l.2149–2155). This process may then be mirrored in the individuals who either read or actively work with the stories and characters. It is also evident in the ten stories in this collection:

1. *The Glow Fish* focuses on attachment and separation. It tells the story of a new species of fish, born in a tiny pond under the shade of a willow tree. When the fish outgrow their home and cry out for help, three water spirits come to their aid and invite them to move to either the river, ocean or lake. The story explores the challenge of moving forward when feeling trapped or stuck; the excitement and fear that potential growth and freedom may induce; the pressure to move out (or to move on) due to circumstances beyond one's control. For some, it may symbolise the journey from childhood through to adolescence and adulthood, or the dilemma of whether to move forward as an individual or to remain attached to a family unit or group. It also allows for an exploration of different personality types.

2. *The Lost One* works particularly well with an individual, though it can also be used with a group. The protagonist is a character named Perdu (the French word for lost), who can be either male or female. She is trapped and has forgotten who she is, remembering only her name. She is afraid to look back, to live truly in the present, or to look forward. Symbolically, her mental state has echoes of depression, anxiety disorder, grief, disassociation and unprocessed trauma. There are four enchanted doors in the room in which Perdu 'sleeps', who decide to wake her up. While externalised as characters in the story, they may represent different aspects of her psyche or unconscious.

3. *Guardian of Dogs* is the story of five dogs, whose different experiences have pushed them out of human society. Together they form a new pack and embark upon a search for the Guardian, a mythical dog who they hope can help them. Themes of rejection, neglect, abuse, abandonment and bereavement are introduced through the five canine characters' substories. Their journey then brings trust, recovery and hope. As with every story in this collection, there is no clear ending and individuals are encouraged to decide how the Guardian of Dogs can help the five travellers, how the story will end or where the next step of their journey will lead.

4. *Boy in a Tree* was inspired by my teenage nephew, who has autistic spectrum disorder and feels most at ease when sitting high in the branches of a tree. At times, he also chooses to sleep through the day and remain awake at night, to avoid the many things he does not understand and finds challenging. There are many people

who feel overwhelmed by day-to-day life and would at times prefer to avoid it. This story explores themes of avoidance, self-preservation, relationships, communication, adolescence, fear, courage and the potential for change.

5. *Little Blue* explores several themes: immigration, family expectations, relationships, prejudice and betrayal. It is the tale of Kororā (the Māori name for the little blue penguin), whose ancestors have travelled across the Indian Ocean to make a new home on the South African coast. The story begins with her birth, then moves to her first day of hunting and her secret friendship with Dapper, a black-footed penguin from the native colony on the other side of the beach.

6. *The Glass Wall* is about confinement and freedom, attachment and separation. The central character is a young otter named Fidget, who is desperate to escape from an aquarium. There are two other characters, who have formed an attachment to Fidget and fear for his survival: Jenna, a shy young woman who prefers the company of animals to humans; and his surrogate mother Lyla, an older female otter in the aquarium. One of the questions at the end of the story is: How do we know when we are ready for the next step of our journey and how difficult is it to move away from (or let go of) people or places to which we feel attached?

7. *Silver Angel* is the story of a unique friendship that develops between a lonely butterfly and a frustrated caterpillar. Together they transform and their journey addresses the importance of friendship and the impact of loss.

8. *Born of Shadow and Light* features two central characters, who may symbolise two halves of the same person, or perhaps two individuals: one who has suppressed their 'shadow part', in an effort to experience life with less pain; the other who is overly connected to their 'shadow parts' and is therefore unable to experience the lighter, brighter aspects of life. The story is essentially about working towards inner balance and may be considered in relation to Jungian psychology. Jung hypothesised that in addition to our Core Self, we each contain the following archetypal parts: Ego, Persona, Shadow and Anima or Animus. By understanding and accepting these parts, people may be able to live a more genuine and fulfilling life.

9. *Survivors* is set in a garden that offers protection to creatures hiding from the outside world. Here, they rebuild their confidence and find the inner strength and courage they need to continue their lives. The idea is that by connecting to these attributes, individuals can allow themselves to be visible, despite the trauma (or other challenging life experiences) they have endured. The garden may represent either an internal or a physical place and the challenge is to take refuge when needed and then know how and when to step outside again.

10. *Nature's Spirits* encourages people to explore and express their individuality, while also considering themselves in relation to others and the world at large. Current environmental issues, including global warming, deforestation and pollution, are

gently introduced, as the story follows a group of young nature spirits, who must leave Aether, the wise and spiritual, to travel across the ancient, elemental realms of Earth, Fire, Water and Air. This final story mirrors aspects of the first story in the collection, *The Glow Fish*. It also ends with the young spirits remembering Aether's advice, that they must each find their own way – words that are found in the collection's title and which encapsulate the theme that flows through all ten stories.

How to use this resource

Life can be immensely challenging and there are significant things that remain out of our control: the social and cultural circumstances into which we are born, our genetic make-up, the traumas and losses we encounter, etc. Essential rules and structures also exist throughout society, even at home. Schools, colleges, hospitals and prisons, for example, rely on specific rules and boundaries, and when freedom is limited it becomes increasingly important to offer choice wherever possible. The stories and activities in this collection aim to encourage young people to explore choices and possibilities, despite the things they cannot control or the limitations they encounter.

Choosing a story

Your choice of story should be based on the needs of your students or clients. Consider what themes are most relevant to them at present or which of the stories is most likely to interest or inspire them.

Each story has a clear theme indicated beside its title. You can read through the brief summaries offered earlier in this chapter, or for more information a detailed introduction precedes each story in the following ten chapters. Below is a quick reference list of the titles and themes:

1. *The Glow Fish* — Attachment, separation and personality types
2. *The Lost One* — Past, future, present
3. *Guardian of Dogs* — Rejection, abuse, trust and recovery
4. *Boy in a Tree* — Avoidance, self-preservation, fear and courage
5. *Little Blue* — Immigration, expectations, relationships and prejudice
6. *The Glass Wall* — Confinement and freedom, attachment and separation
7. *Silver Angel* — Friendship, transformation and loss
8. *Born of Shadow and Light* — Emotional balance
9. *Survivors* — Inner strength and courage
10. *Nature's Spirits* — Environmental issues and personality types

Introducing the stories

The way you introduce a story depends on several key factors:

1. The needs and abilities of your students or clients.
2. Your professional role, unique skill set, experience and personality.
3. The goals or focus you have identified for the story work.
4. Your relationship with the group or individual.

Here are some useful tips:

▶ Trust in your abilities and professional judgement, then consider the most appropriate way to begin. Teachers, dramatherapists, storytellers and counsellors, for example, will all approach this work very differently, yet all methods are valid and potentially beneficial.

▶ Each story is preceded by an introduction, which may give you some ideas. Also, familiarise yourself with a new story before introducing it to a group or individual.

▶ Explain that the story is open to interpretation, followed by choices rather than a definite ending.

▶ If it's appropriate, offer everyone a copy of the narrative. While some people may prefer to actively listen, others will find it helpful to follow a text. Whatever their preference, it will probably be useful to have a written copy of the story to refer to at a later stage of the process. Copies of each of the stories are available at www.pavpub.com/find-your-way-resources, from where they can be printed as needed.

▶ Whenever possible, actively involve people in the storytelling process. Ask if anyone would like to read out part of the story, for example, such as one of the character's short monologues. You can also introduce simple props to bring the story to life when first sharing it. This will be particularly helpful for those who are unable to work with a written text. Also, encourage your students or clients to consider how the story makes them feel, or what it makes them think about.

▶ Individuals will respond differently to each story and you cannot anticipate every response. Therefore, remain attentive, ready to work with any thoughts, feelings, associations or themes that may arise.

▶ Finally, establish a non-judgemental environment in which your students or clients feel able to express their themselves freely and creatively.

Using the creative activities

Several creative activities are described in relation to each of the stories in the book. They have all been used successfully with groups and most can be adapted for individual work:

Here are some useful tips:

▶ Discussion is often the most effective way to begin.
▶ You do not have to introduce every activity described.

- You do not have to follow the order in which the activities are listed.
- You can add your own activities or adapt those suggested to suit your needs.
- The main activities include:
  - discussion (with guided questions and choices)
  - hot seating
  - improvisation
  - dramatic tableaus
  - artwork
  - creative writing
  - script work
- Whenever possible, allow the energy, nature and initial response of a group or individual to guide you, helping you to choose the most effective creative activities to develop the work further.
- While some people enjoy participating in script work, for example, others will prefer the freedom of improvisation. Offering a mix of creative activities will allow individuals to express themselves through a variety of media. They may find some more challenging than others. If you offer support and encouragement, however, the process can be liberating.
- If you have a clear goal or focus and want to steer your students or clients in a specific direction, you can also plan which activities to use with your chosen story and allocate a set number of lessons or sessions for the creative work.

Most importantly, maintain a positive environment in which your students or clients know that there is no right or wrong response to any story or creative activity. Your goal is to encourage the young people you are working with to explore positive choices and possibilities, despite the aspects of life that challenge them or remain out of their control.

References

All-Party Parliamentary Group on Arts, Health and Wellbeing – APPGAHW (2017a) *Creative Health: The Arts for Health and Wellbeing – Inquiry Report* (2nd edition). London: All-Party Parliamentary Group on Arts, Health and Wellbeing. Available from https://www.culturehealthandwellbeing.org.uk/appg-inquiry/

All-Party Parliamentary Group on Arts, Health and Wellbeing – APPGAHW (2017b) *Policy Briefing: Arts Engagement and Wellbeing*. London: All-Party Parliamentary Group on Arts, Health and Wellbeing, produced in partnership with What Works Centre for Wellbeing.

Baum FL (1900) *The Wonderful Wizard of Oz*. Illustrated by WW Denslow. Chicago: George M. Hill Company.

British Association of Dramatherapists – BADth (2020) Dramatherapy. Available at http://badth.org.uk/dtherapy

Campbell J with Moyers B (1991) *The Power of Myth* (Kindle edition). New York: Anchor Books.

Carroll L (1865) *The Adventures of Alice in Wonderland*. Illustrated by J Tenniel. London: Macmillan.

Erikson MH & Rosen S (1991) *My Voice Will Go with You: Teaching Tales of Milton H. Erickson*. Reprint edition. New York: W. W. Norton & Company.

Feltman CE & Szymanski DM (2018) Instagram Use and Self-objectification: The Roles of Internalization, Comparison, Appearance Commentary, and Feminism. *Sex Roles* **78** 311–324. doi: 10.1007/s11199-017-0796-1.

Gersie A (1997) *Reflections on Therapeutic Storymaking: The Use of Stories in Groups* (Kindle edition). London and Philadelphia: Jessica Kingsley Publishers.

Hillman J (1997) *Re-visioning Psychology*. Reissue edition. New York: William Morrow Paperbacks.

HCPC – Health and Care Professions Council (2013) Standards of Proficiency – Arts Therapists. Available at: https://www.hcpcuk.org/globalassets/resources/standards/standards-of-proficiency---arts-therapists.pdf

HM Government (2019) *Online Harms – White Paper*. Presented to Parliament by the Secretary of State for Digital, Culture, Media & Sport and the Secretary of State for the Home Department by Command of Her Majesty. Printed in the UK by the APS Group on behalf of the Controller of Her Majesty's Stationery Office. © Crown Copyright 2019. Available at: www.gov.uk/government/publications

Jennings S (2016) Foreword. In: Jennings S and Holmwood C (eds) *Routledge International Handbook of Dramatherapy* (Routledge International Handbooks). Kindle edition. Taylor and Francis.

Jennings S (2007) Interview with Sue Jennings. In: Jones P (ed) *Drama as Therapy Volume 1: Theory, Practice and Research*. Second edition. Kindle edition. Routledge (Taylor & Francis Group).

Jennings S (1990) *Dramatherapy with Families, Groups and Individuals*. London: Jessica Kingsley Publishers.

Jones P (2007) *Drama as Therapy Volume 1: Theory, Practice and Research* (2nd edition) (Kindle edition). London: Taylor & Francis.

Jung CG (1968) *The Archetypes and the Collective Unconscious* (2nd edition) (Kindle edition). London: Taylor & Francis.

Lahad M (2013) Six Parts Story revisited. The seven levels of assessment drawn from the 6 PSM. In: M Lahad, M Shacham and O Ayalon (Eds) *The 'BASIC PH' Model of Coping and Resiliency: Theory, Research and Cross-Cultural Application*. London: Jessica Kingsley Publishers.

Levine SK (2005) The philosophy of expressive arts therapy: poiesis as a response to the world. In: Paolo J Knill, Ellen G Levine & SK Levine (Eds) *Principles and Practice of Expressive Arts Therapy: Toward a Therapeutic Aesthetic*. London and Philadelphia: Jessica Kingsley Publishers.

Lindkvist M (2007) Interview with (Marian) Billy Lindkvist. In: Jones P (ed.) *Drama as Therapy Volume 1: Theory, Practice and Research*. Second edition (Kindle edition). Routledge (Taylor & Francis Group).

May R (1991) *The Cry for Myth*. New York: Dell Publishing.

Mental Health Foundation (2019) Who we are and what we do. Available at: https://www.mentalhealth.org.uk/about-us/who-we-are

Milne AA (1926) *Winnie-the-Pooh*. Illustrated by EH Shepard. London: Methuen and Co. Ltd.

Mir E and Novas C (2017) Social Media and Adolescents' and Young Adults' Mental Health. *National Center for Health Research*. Available at: http://www.center4research.org/social-media-affects-mental-health/

Morris S (2018) *Dramatherapy for Borderline Personality Disorder: Empowering and Nurturing People through Creativity*. Oxon and New York: Routledge.

NHS – National Health Service, UK (2019) *The NHS Long Term Plan*. Available at: https://www.longtermplan.nhs.uk/publication/nhs-long-term-plan/

Nongard R & Hazlerig MA (2014) *Speak Ericksonian: Mastering the Hypnotic Methods of Milton Erickson* (Kindle edition). Arizona: Peachtree Professional Education, Inc.

Parkinson R (2009) *Transforming Tales: How Stories Can Change People*. London and Philadelphia: Jessica Kingsley Publishers.

Primack BA, Shensa A, Sidani JE, Whaite EO, Lin L, Rosen D, Colditz JB, Radovic A & Miller E (2017) Social Media Use and Perceived Social Isolation among Young Adults. *American Journal of Preventive Medicine* **53** (1) 1–8. DOI:10.1016/j.amepre.2017.01.010.

Schrader C (2012) Myth-a-drama. In *Ritual Theatre: The Power of Dramatic Ritual in Personal Development Groups and Clinical Practice* (Kindle edition). London and Philadelphia: Jessica Kingsley Publishers.

Shensa A, Escobar-Viera C, Sidani J, Bowman M, Marshal M & Primack B (2017) Problematic Social Media Use and Depressive Symptoms among U.S. Young Adults: A Nationally-Representative Study. *Social Science & Medicine* **182** 150–157.

Smail M (2000) *Psyche and Soma* at SoulWorks 2020 – Soul Making through the Sesame approach. Available at: www.marysmailsoulworks.co.uk/courses/18-psyche-and-soma-2020 (accessed April 2020).

Smail M (2016) Open Sesame and the Soul Cave. In: Jennings S and Holmwood C (editors) *Routledge International Handbook of Dramatherapy* (Routledge International Handbooks). Kindle edition. Taylor and Francis.

Van der Kolk B (2015) Chapter 20: Finding Your Voice: Communal Rhythms and Theater. In: *The Body Keeps the Score*. London: Penguin Books, Random House.

WHO – World Health Organisation (2019) *Suicide Fact Sheet*. Available at: https://www.who.int/news-room/fact-sheets/detail/suicide

Yalom I (2008) *Staring at the Sun: Overcoming the Dread of Death* (Kindle edition). London: Hachette Digital.

Story 1

The Glow Fish

Attachment, separation and personality types

Illustration by Nicky Morris

Introduction

The Glow Fish is suitable for both individual and group work. It explores several themes: the challenge of moving forward when feeling 'stuck', making significant decisions, independent thinking, the excitement and fear that potential growth and freedom may induce, the concept of choice, the pressure to move out (or to move on) due to circumstances beyond one's control, the journey from childhood through to adolescence then adulthood, and the dilemma of whether to move forward as an individual or to remain attached to a family unit or group. It may also touch on other issues, such as being (or feeling) different or exposed.

The Glow Fish should appeal to a variety of people, of different ages, genders, cultures, etc. For professionals, it could be used as a creative tool through which to assess the current mood and mental state of one's clients or students. For example, the facilitator would note the way in which each person responds to the story: the parts they choose, the themes they identify and the choices they make. It may also reveal the participants' ability to self-reflect and to imagine a future for themselves. If presenting the story to a group, it will help individual members to make sense of themselves and others, while group dynamics can be safely explored through metaphor.

An enactment of *The Glow Fish* could involve several performers. Eight characters are indicated in the mini script: Willow Tree (who acts as narrator and could be a shared part), four Glow Fish (a number which could be extended or reduced) and three Water Spirits. With no definitive ending, the story (and mini script) offer the opportunity for discussion, improvisation and/or creative writing. There is also the potential to add music and/or artwork. Individuals may choose (and alternate) between roles. Most significantly, they should be encouraged to create their own ending. The story can be considered as a starting point and the mini script that follows as an additional resource used to initiate enactment when improvisation is perhaps too daunting. By working through the process (over one or several sessions), individuals should be encouraged to find their own meaning in the story – from both a personal and a group perspective.

The Glow Fish (narrative)[1]

In a tiny pond, under the shade of sighing willow tree, a new species of fish was born.

The Glow Fish were delicate, sensitive and impressionable. They grew fast in body and spirit. Soon, they felt constricted and confined. They cried into the murky water that now barely contained them, gasping for air, desperate for help.

As their tears evaporated into the warm sky above, their cries were heard by three Water Spirits. Each were passionate about their watery homes, keen to attract new life and determined to persuade the Glow Fish to leave their pond and reside with them. Spiralling through a fountain of ice-cold water, the Spirit of the River arrived first. Young and excitable, she spoke in an alluring, enticing tone:

'My river is full of life. It flows with the wind, constantly moving, offering a distinct path to follow. Live in my river and you will never grow weary of your surroundings, as they

---

* The text of this story can be downloaded and printed at www.pavpub.com/find-your-way-resources

will constantly change. The cleansing rush of water will lead you to so many places, countless streams and adventures. You will remain free, staying close to the land, while drenched in my tantalising waters.'

The Glow Fish responded to her words with excitement, imagining the river as their new home. Preparing to leave the confines of their pond, heavy storm clouds suddenly emerged. A torrent of rain began to pour, through which the Spirit of the Ocean appeared, majestic and powerful. As she spoke, the rain ceased, the dark clouds clearing as swiftly as they had formed. Her words were persuasive, her tone brimming with authority and strength:

'My ocean is mysterious and vast, offering you a world of opportunity and choice. Find the courage to join me and you will develop the strength to conquer anything. My waters offer the most challenging, complex and rewarding journey. If you dare to join me, you will learn to overcome all that stands in your way. You will sink to the depths, then rise and ride the waves.'

The Glow Fish were in awe of this powerful Spirit and her passionate words. Some felt drawn to the journey she offered, while others were afraid. This led to a fracture in their family – born as one, yet now experiencing opposing thoughts and feelings for the first time. As the conversation moved back and forth between them, a shimmering fog formed around their pond and the graceful Spirit of the Lake glided into view. She spoke in peaceful, reflective tones:

'My lake is beautiful, yet dark and deep. Today, you are challenged with a significant choice and life will continue to demand such profound decisions. The still waters of my lake will gently wash over you, offering the time and space you need for deep thought, emotion and introspection. Look into my waters and you will find your answers. Look within and you will know which path to choose. You may travel together; you may travel alone. Trust in your instincts and swim.'

The Glow Fish watched in wonder as the serene Spirit of the Lake glided back into the fog from which she came. The air was silent and still. They knew they must soon decide their fate. The river, the ocean and the lake were calling them. Their suffocating pond, once a perfect cocoon, could no longer sustain them and the shade of the willow tree would no longer protect them.

The Glow Fish understood the significance of their choice. Must they separate and take individual paths, or could they remain together? There was uncertainty between them and while a few were excited, others were unsure and some frightened. They knew they must now look within, as the Spirit of the Lake had suggested, though did not know what they would discover.

The story pauses here

*Now, imagine you are a Glow Fish, ready to begin your new life.
Would you follow the free and flowing Spirit of the River,
the mighty Spirit of the Ocean or the wise Spirit of the Lake?*

Their story has no definitive ending, only questions with answers to be found.

The choice is yours.

Story 1: The Glow Fish

Creative activities

Several activities can be offered in relation to *The Glow Fish*, and new activities may also be created. The list below describes key exercises that have been used successfully with groups, and some can be adapted for individual work. You do not have to introduce every activity, nor follow the order in which they are listed. Discussion, however, is often an effective way to begin. The energy or nature of a group (or an individual's initial response to the story) will also guide you towards the most appropriate and effective way of working with it. Some people enjoy participating in script work, for example, while others may prefer the freedom of improvisation. On the other hand, you might have selected this story in order to steer your students or clients in a specific direction – to encourage creative writing, for example. There is no right or wrong way to work with the story, just as there is no right or wrong choice for the Glow Fish to make.

Discussion and choices

After sharing the story with a group, ask them to move into pairs or small groups and encourage them to discuss what they thought about the story and to decide which Water Spirit they would choose to follow and why. Each person can also select a line from the story that makes an impact on them. After these discussions, bring the group back together and invite everyone to share their thoughts. If the group is working in pairs, one approach is to ask each member to say what their partner decided and why. If working with an individual, adapt the process accordingly. It is also important to remember that the choices people make at this point may reflect something significant about their current mood and mental state, or memories.

Dramatic landscapes

The three Water Spirits offer the Glow Fish different water landscapes, which are symbolic of varying states of mind or thought processes. Ask the members of your group to choose which of the Water Spirits they would follow, then invite them to form mini groups based on their choices: River, Ocean or Lake. In these groups, participants can work together to create a dramatic tableau (defined as a group of motionless figures representing a scene) representing their chosen water landscape. They can do this using their bodies. Voice can also be used, adding words or sound effects, and the tableaus can be either still or moving. If props are available, a selection of material (different colours and textures), masks, percussive instruments, etc. could be useful. When ready, the groups should be encouraged to show one another their dramatic landscapes.

Artwork

Invite the members of your group (or the individual with whom you're working) to create their own Glow Fish. They can do this using whatever arts and crafts materials are available and their creative piece can be either 2D or 3D. Templates could also be offered, or chosen online, if there is access to a PC and printer. If working in a group, participants should be encouraged to show one another their individual Glow Fish when ready.

Creative writing

A helpful strategy to introduce creative writing is to ask an individual (or members of a group) to imagine what would happen if the story were to continue. There are many possibilities. Should the group of Glow Fish remain together, for example, or separate and move in different directions? If they separate, will they ever see each other again, and is it possible to move between the three water landscapes offered? Alternatively, they could also focus on the continuing journey of a single Glow Fish, rather than write about the whole group. Creative writing can be in either narrative or script form, and works equally well with an individual or group.

Improvisation

There are three Water Spirits and a fluid number of Glow Fish, which can be explored and brought to life through improvisation. Depending on the size of a group, participants could take turns to play the three Water Spirits, or they could form mini groups. The Willow Tree could also be dramatised, symbolising a parental figure or used as a narrator, as in the mini script that follows. Props, costume and sound effects may be added to enhance the process.

The Glow Fish (mini script)

Eight characters are named; however, this could be adjusted to suit the size of any group, by either sharing parts or splitting into smaller groups, etc. The Willow Tree is included as the story's narrator. **Willow Tree** (Narrator), **Glow Fish 1** (confident), **Glow Fish 2** (enthusiastic), **Glow Fish 3** (worried), **Glow Fish 4** (supportive), **Spirit of the River** (young and excited), **Sprit of the Ocean** (majestic and strong), **Spirit of the Lake** (wise and graceful):

Willow Tree:	In a tiny pond, under the safety of my branches, the Glow Fish were born. They were delicate, sensitive and impressionable. They grew fast in body and spirit, soon feeling constricted and confined.
Glow Fish 1:	What's happening?
Glow Fish 2:	We need more space.
Glow Fish 3:	We need more light.
Glow Fish 4:	We need help!
Willow Tree:	They cried into the murky water of their pond, gasping for air, desperate for help.

Story 1: The Glow Fish

Glow Fish 1:	Help us!
Glow Fish 2:	We've no space to swim.
Glow Fish 3:	We're struggling to breathe.
Glow Fish 4:	Help us, please!
Willow Tree:	Their tears evaporated into the warm sky above and their cries were heard by three Water Spirits. Each passionate about their watery homes, they were determined to persuade the Glow Fish to leave their pond and live with them. Spiralling through a fountain of ice-cold water, the excitable Spirit of the River arrived first!
Spirit of the River:	*(Young and excitable, she speaks in an alluring, enticing tone.)* Have no fear, I can help you! My river is full of life. It flows with the wind, constantly moving, offering a distinct path to follow. Live in my river and you will never grow weary of your surroundings, as they will constantly change.
Glow Fish 1:	It sounds wonderful!
Glow Fish 2:	Yes, we will swim like the wind, with all the space we need.
Glow Fish 3:	Are we sure it's safe?
Glow Fish 4:	If we stay together, nothing can harm us.
Spirit of the River:	Come with me now! The cleansing rush of water will lead you to so many places, countless streams and adventures. You will remain forever free, staying close to the land, while drenched in my tantalising waters.
Willow Tree:	The Glow Fish were excited, imagining the river as their new home. They felt ready to leave the pond and to follow the Spirit of the River.
Glow Fish 1:	Let's go!
Glow Fish 2:	There's no time to lose.
Glow Fish 3:	I think I'm ready!
Glow Fish 4:	Just stay close to me.
Willow Tree:	Just as they prepared to leave, heavy storm clouds suddenly emerged and a torrent of rain began to pour. The majestic Spirit of the Ocean appeared before them. She spoke and the rain ceased, the dark clouds clearing as swiftly as they had formed.
Spirit of the Ocean:	*(Majestic, powerful and persuasive, she speaks with strength and authority.)*

Story 1: The Glow Fish

	Do not be so hasty! Before you follow my sister to the River, you must consider my Ocean. It is mysterious and vast, offering you a world of opportunity and choice. Find the courage to join me and you will develop the strength to conquer anything.
Glow Fish 1:	I want to be strong!
Glow Fish 2:	I want to be courageous!
Glow Fish 3:	I just want to be safe.
Glow Fish 4:	We must simply stay together.
Spirit of the Ocean:	My waters offer the most challenging, complex and rewarding journey. If you dare to join me, you will learn to overcome all that stands in your way. You will sink to the depths, then rise up and ride the waves!
Willow Tree:	The Glow Fish were in awe of this powerful Spirit and her passionate words. Some felt drawn to the journey she offered, while others were afraid. This led to the first fracture in their family – born as one, yet now experiencing opposing thoughts and feelings for the first time.
Glow Fish 1:	The Ocean is for me!
Glow Fish 2:	Yet the River runs so free!
Glow Fish 3:	The Ocean is too vast, the River too fast. I want to stay where I am.
Glow Fish 4:	If we move in different directions, what will become of us?
Willow Tree:	As the conversation moved back and forth between them, a shimmering fog formed around their pond and the graceful Spirit of the Lake glided into view.
Spirit of the Lake:	*(She is graceful and speaks in peaceful, reflective tones.)* Be still for a moment, my friends. Before you follow my sisters, you should consider my Lake. It is beautiful, yet dark and deep. Today, you are challenged with a significant choice and life will continue to demand such decisions. The still waters of my Lake will gently wash over you, offering the time and space needed for deep thought, emotion and introspection.
Glow Fish 1:	She is so wise, yet the Ocean still calls me.
Glow Fish 2:	I am tempted, yet the rush of the River pulls me.
Glow Fish 3:	I don't know what to do, I'm not sure what I feel.
Glow Fish 4:	I want to move on to new waters, though not alone.

Spirit of the Lake:	Look into my waters and you will find your answers. Look within and you will know which path to choose. You may travel together; you may travel alone. Trust in your instincts and swim.
Willow Tree:	The Glow Fish watched in wonder as the serene Spirit of the Lake glided back into the fog from which she came. The air was silent and still. They knew they must soon decide their fate. Their suffocating pond, once a perfect cocoon, could no longer sustain them and my branches could no longer protect them.
Glow Fish 1:	We must leave the pond!
Glow Fish 2:	Yes, it's time. Take courage and choose your own paths.
Glow Fish 3:	I'm afraid. What if I get lost?
Glow Fish 4:	If we separate, stay strong.
Glow Fish 2:	We won't forget each other and one day we may reunite.
Willow Tree:	The Glow Fish understood the significance of their choice. Some would travel alone, while others might stay together. They looked at one another, then up to my branches and beyond. Finally, they looked within, and each then swam in their chosen direction.

Examples of work in practice

You may discover that while some clients enjoy having a copy of the story to follow, others prefer to relax and listen. Likewise, some might respond well to script work and others will favour a freer, more spontaneous approach. As reflective discussions develop among one group, another will choose to remain in the creative realm. Just as the Glow Fish are offered three new homes to choose between, choice is the prevailing element here. It is imperative that everyone is heard and their choices are respected. In a group, this could prove challenging at times, and as a facilitator one should try to be as flexible as possible, while encouraging compromise and finding the most appropriate method with which to proceed. *The Glow Fish* has been introduced to many people – men and women, teenagers and adults. A few key examples follow. Pseudonyms are used when referring to clients:

Young women with psychosis

For the last ten years, I have worked in a therapeutic step-down service for women with a range of mental health difficulties, predominantly psychotic disorders such as schizophrenia. In the NICE guideline for psychosis, it is advised that as well as CBT and family therapy, arts therapies should be considered for all individuals with psychotic disorders, ideally in group format, using a combination of psychotherapeutic techniques and activities that encourage creative expression (2014, p26). NICE clarifies that arts therapy sessions can be offered during an acute phase of a psychotic illness. They also indicate three key aims, which correspond with my approach:

'1.) Helping individuals to experience themselves anew, whilst introducing alternative methods of communication. 2.) Encouraging self-expression, framed within a positive creative form. 3.) Helping them to accept and understand the feelings that surface within sessions, when appropriate.' (NICE, 2014, p26).

As previously written about my work on this unit, 'Freedom, choice and acceptance … are themes that often arise and Dramatherapy provides the women with a space in which to safely voice their frustrations and celebrate their individuality' (Morris, 2018, p114). This client group have benefited considerably from the new stories, mini scripts and activities in this collection. *The Glow Fish* was the first of the stories in this collection to be introduced and has since been used with several women in this setting. The following examples show how the original clients responded to it. Pseudonyms are used.

1. **Tina** was in her early 30s, with medication-resistant paranoid schizophrenia. She was a regular member of the group. Her mood was quite subdued this week and she was observed to quietly talk to herself during much of the hour. In contrast, when reading the roles of the 'Spirit of the Ocean' and the 'Spirit of the River', she was able to focus completely. She found it difficult to reflect on the themes and choices offered, however, explaining that she had other thoughts in her head.

2. **Bailey** was in her early 30s, with medication-resistant schizophrenia. She was dedicated to the Dramatherapy group, though at times avoided participating in certain activities due to her spiritual beliefs and OCD. She was keen to attend the first *Glow Fish* session and engaged throughout with focus and interest. Her mood remained bright and she interacted well with her peers, sharing that her spiritual name was 'River' and that she felt most connected to the 'Spirit of the River'.

3. **Kitty** was in her 30s, with medication-resistant schizophrenia. She was a loyal member of the Dramatherapy group and keen to attend this session. Her mood appeared bright and her mental state stable. She responded positively to the new story and offered to read the part of the 'Spirit of the Ocean' in both the narrative and mini script. Kitty showed interest in the ideas and choices shared by her peers and interacted well with them.

4. **Sarah** was in her early 20s, diagnosed with schizophrenia. She was a regular member of the Dramatherapy group and keen to attend the first *Glow Fish* session. She engaged in every activity with focus and enthusiasm, responding positively to the new story. She offered to take the part of the 'Spirit of the River' during the initial reading of the narrative and chose to play the 'Willow Tree' (narrator) when the mini script was read. She interacted well with her peers; her mood remained bright and her mental state stable.

Young women with EUPD

For the past 15 years I have worked on low secure wards, offering specialist treatment to women diagnosed with EUPD (emotionally unstable personality disorder) also known as BPD (borderline personality disorder). The DBT (dialectical behavioural therapy) programme is complemented by OT (occupational therapy) and Dramatherapy. As described in an earlier article of mine, 'Whilst DBT offers the patients concrete ideas and coping strategies, Dramatherapy allows them to play and to express the unsaid' (Morris, 2014, p4). I began to write the stories in this collection to help me to connect with a group of particularly complex (and unusually withdrawn) service users.

In June 2015, NICE released a new quality standard (QS88) to improve the treatment and care of people with BPD in the UK, advocating flexible, person-centred psychological therapies. Dramatherapy meets these criteria, offering an empowering process with unique structures that can both embrace and contain the emotional chaos often experienced by people with BPD. The NHS currently includes the Arts Therapies (art therapy, dance movement therapy, Dramatherapy and music therapy) as one of five treatment choices for BPD (2020) and they were listed among the 10 most relevant approaches to support people with the diagnosis in the UK Department of Health's handbook (DH, 2014, p80). NICE also acknowledges the prevalence and relevance of arts therapies in BPD treatment programmes and therapeutic communities. They are not yet included in their concise guideline, however, due to a lack of quantitative research such as RCTs (2009, pp115–117).

This client group has benefited significantly from the new stories, mini scripts and activities in the collection. *The Glow Fish* was the first original story written. It was explored over three sessions, using a range of dramatic activities and artwork. The following examples show how different clients responded to it. Pseudonyms are used.

1. **Lara** was 18 years old and very far from home. She attended all three sessions.

   Session 1 – Lara had recently been admitted to the ward and this was her first Dramatherapy group. She shared initially that she was settling in okay, though feeling very homesick. She engaged fully in every activity and responded positively to the new story. She felt most connected to the Spirit of the River, who offered freedom. Lara was also able to relate the story to her own difficult experience of leaving home and being admitted to the ward.

   Session 2 – Lara came willingly and engaged fully. At times, physical symptoms of anxiety were evident. During the script work undertaken, however, she relaxed and appeared confident. She chose to take on the role of the 'enthusiastic' Glow Fish who feels drawn to the river. She read her part with expression and confidence. She also worked expressively with her chosen ribbon wand during the final enactment.

   Session 3 – Lara came willingly and engaged well. She shared initially that she was feeling very tired. In response to the theme, she created her own Glow Fish, who she said was keen to swim to the river. She said at the end that although she remained tired, she had enjoyed the session.

2. **Rachel** had recently been diagnosed with ASD (autistic spectrum disorder), as well as having EUPD. She was 19 years old and attended all three sessions.

   Session 1 – Rachel said initially that she was feeling very tired and her weekend had been terrible. She engaged fully in all parts of the session, however, and responded positively to the new story. She felt most connected to the Spirit of the Ocean, who offered the opportunity to learn to overcome all that stands in one's way. Rachel then showed creativity and a sense of play, when creating an ocean tableau with her partner. At the end of the session, she said she was pleased to have come.

Session 2 – Rachel came willingly and shared initially that she was feeling 'agitated'. Despite this, she engaged fully in every activity. During the scripted enactment of *The Glow Fish* she chose to be the 'confident' Glow Fish, who feels drawn to the ocean. She read the part expressively and said at the end that although she still felt agitated, she had enjoyed the experience.

Session 3 – Rachel came willingly and engaged fully. She chose to say very little, but immersed herself in the creative process, making her own delicate Glow Fish using art materials.

3. **Anya** had complex difficulties, having previously endured a severe psychotic episode that led to her taking an overdose, resulting in a coma. She had since had intense physiotherapy and was on the ward to receive psychological treatment for EUPD. She attended two of the three sessions.

    Session 1 – Anya shared initially that while she was feeling okay, she had not felt like attending any groups today. She had come, however, after applying the 'opposite action' – a DBT emotion regulation skill. She engaged fully in every activity and responded positively to the new story. She felt most connected to the Spirit of the Lake, who offered the safest, most peaceful home. Anya also identified the theme of growing away from people and taking separate paths. She said at the end that she was pleased to have come.

    Session 3 – Anya had missed the Dramatherapy group the previous day due to a dental appointment. She came to this session willingly, however, despite struggling with tooth pain. She acknowledged the need for positive distraction and immersed herself in the creative process. In response to the theme, she used art materials to create her own Glow Fish, who she described as very young. She named her Leela and said she understood that life was going to have to change, though felt unsure how she would cope with this. Anya said at the end that she had enjoyed the session, despite the pain distracting her.

4. **Sarah** was 20 years old. She suffered from oppressive depression and EUPD. She was often very flat in affect (with an apparent absence of emotional response, her voice and face showing little expression). Through story and script work, however, her demeanour changed. She attended all three sessions.

    Session 1 – Sarah was feeling extremely tired, having slept badly the previous two nights. She managed to participate, although her mood remained subdued much of the time. In response to the new story, she felt most connected to the Spirit of the River, who offered adventure.

Story 1: The Glow Fish

Session 2 – Sarah was the first to choose a role in the scripted enactment of the story, taking on the part of the 'worried' Glow Fish. She read expressively and said at the end that she had enjoyed the experience.

Session 3 – Sarah appeared quite bright in mood and responded expressively to the activity of creating her own Glow Fish with art materials. She explained that her Glow Fish did not want to leave the pond and was fearful of change.

5. **Tracey** was in her early 20s and diagnosed with EUPD. She attended all three sessions.

Session 1 – Tracey came willingly and shared initially that she was feeling 'quite good'. She engaged in every activity and responded positively to the new story. She offered to read the part of one of the three Water Spirits in the narrative and later said she felt most drawn to the Spirit of the Lake. She then showed initiative and creativity when creating a lake tableau with her partner, and said at the end that she had enjoyed the group.

Session 2 – Tracey came willingly and engaged fully in the warm-up activities. Soon after, however, her mood shifted and she asked to be excused. She returned to the group approximately 10 minutes later, having taken medication. Although her mood appeared subdued, she agreed to participate and took on the role of the 'Spirit of the Ocean' in the scripted enactment of *The Glow Fish*. At the end of the session, her effort to return to the group and participate, despite struggling, was acknowledged.

Session 3 – Tracey came willingly and engaged fully. She created a vibrant Glow Fish using art materials and said that she felt happier than usual with her finished piece. The significance of this was then acknowledged, as self-criticism was an ongoing issue for Tracey.

6. **Mary** was in her early 20s and diagnosed with EUPD. She also struggled to distinguish between reality and fiction at times. She attended two of the three sessions.

Session 2 – Mary had missed the first session. She attended the second, despite feeling low in mood. She spoke openly about her sadness and appeared to struggle during the first part of the session. When we began working on the new script, she said initially that she did not want to read a part. She then changed her mind and her mood visibly improved as she read the role of the 'Spirit of the River'. She reflected afterwards that she felt far more confident at the end of the session.

Session 3 – Mary came willingly, though shared initially that she was feeling low in mood. She immersed herself in the creative process, however, and used art materials to create her own Glow Fish, whose words were: 'I just want to be free.'

7. **Darla** was in her mid-20s. She was diagnosed with EUPD and was desperate to get well so that she could be discharged and return to her young daughter. She attended two of the three sessions.

   Session 1 – Darla came willingly and engaged fully in all parts the session. She responded positively to the new story and felt most connected to the 'Spirit of the River', who offered a definite path.

   Session 3 – Darla missed the previous day's Dramatherapy group. She came to the expressive session, though shared initially that she was feeling irritated and had not really wanted to come. Despite this, she immersed herself in the creative process, using art materials to create her own Glow Fish, whose words were: 'I am happier to be alone.' Through the activity she had found a way to express herself genuinely, and her effort to attend and participate, despite the way she was feeling, was acknowledged.

Delegates at an annual conference for hypnotherapists

In 2018 I was invited to attend the Hypnotherapy Association's annual conference, to speak about my book *Borderline Personality: Empowering and Nurturing People through Creativity* (Morris, 2018). I also decided to introduce *The Glow Fish* to the delegates, having begun to establish the new stories with my clients, and seeing their potential. I took a variety of props, including different coloured ribbon wands, a rainstick and a thunder stick. Initially I was concerned when one of the delegates asked if we were going to have a children's party. He made several other comments which seemed to have negative connotations.

Thankfully, the interactive presentation went very well and the delegates responded with enthusiasm to *The Glow Fish*. Many of them were keen to choose a ribbon wand or a percussive instrument to use as I shared the story and all of them chose (then discussed) which of the Water Spirits they would follow. After the presentation, the man who had initially caused me concern shared how much he had enjoyed it, particularly the story and all the props. Speaking to him further, I realised that his earlier comments had not been the negative judgements I had perceived them to be and that he had in fact felt excited about the prospect of engaging in something that (to him) resembled a children's party.

This interaction reminded me that things are not always as they seem and that drama, props, stories, etc. can very quickly allow adults to connect to their inner child. At the end of the presentation, many of the delegates asked if they could keep a copy of the *Glow Fish* narrative and mini script, as they were keen to use it in their hypnotherapy practice. Again I was surprised, as I had not yet realised the full potential of the stories and in how many areas they could be used.

When asking the Hypnotherapy Association for feedback to share with reference to *The Glow Fish* (in the context of this publication), Darren Marks, a hypnotherapist and director of the Hypnotherapy Association, wrote the following (2019):

'Nicky Morris was a guest speaker at The Hypnotherapy Association Conference. Her expertise and passion for her subject shone through on every level. The Glow Fish story [which] she related and is to be included in her new book ... inspired many delegates who were then keen to incorporate the metaphor into their own practice. It will be wonderful to have this collection of healing stories gathered together in one place and I would highly recommend them.'

References

DH – Department of Health UK (2014) *Meeting the Challenge, Making a Difference: Working effectively to support people with Personality Disorder in the Community*. Available at: http://www.emergenceplus.org.uk/personality-disorder.html

Marks D (2019) Email with feedback on 'The Glow Fish', in relation to this publication.

Morris N (2014) Silenced in Childhood: A Survivor of Abuse Finds Her Voice through Group Dramatherapy. *Dramatherapy* **36** (1) 3–17.

Morris N (2018) *Dramatherapy for Borderline Personality Disorder: Empowering and Nurturing People through Creativity*. London and New York: Routledge.

NICE (2014) *Psychosis and Schizophrenia in Adults: Prevention and Management* – National Clinical Practice Guideline 178. Available at: www.nice.org.uk/guidance/cg178.

NICE (2015) *Personality Disorders: Borderline and Antisocial: Quality Standard 88*. Available at: www.nice.org.uk/guidance/qs88.

NHS (2020) Arts Therapies. Available at: https://www.nhs.uk/conditions/borderline-personality-disorder/treatment/

Story 2

The Lost One

Past, Future, Present

Illustration by Abbie Stedman

Story 2: The Lost One

Introduction

The Lost One is suitable for both individual and group work. The protagonist is Perdu (who could be either male or female and can be of any age). Perdu (the French word for lost) is trapped and has forgotten who she is, remembering only her name. She is afraid to look back, to live truly in the present, or to look forward. Symbolically, her mental state has echoes of depression, anxiety disorder, grief, dissociation or a response to trauma. The way in which each person responds to her story – the choices they make and the feelings and thoughts it provokes – can help a facilitator to assess their current mood and mental state.

Gersie suggests that in traditional tales, 'Every story character is invited to wake up and to grow up' (1997, p154). This process may then be mirrored in the individuals who either read or actively work with the stories and characters. This translates literally in *The Lost One*, as the enchanted doors in the story invite her to wake from her slumber so that she can either confront her past, step into the present or contemplate her future. Listeners are also invited to imagine themselves in her place.

The Lost One may be reminiscent of three familiar tales: *Sleeping Beauty* (Perrault, 1697), *A Christmas Carol* (Dickens, 1843) and *Rapunzel* (Shultz, 1790). It is however distinctly different and not an adaptation. Unlike Sleeping Beauty, who is awakened by true love's kiss, Perdu responds to a faint desire that stirs deep within – when the four enchanted doors of the room in which she sleeps decide to wake her up. While externalised as characters in the story, they could represent different aspects of her psyche or unconscious.

The group (or individual) working with the story are invited to decide whether Perdu is ready to face her past and, if so, to consider what she might discover. In contrast, they may decide that stepping into a possible future would provide her with the inspiration to move forward. Alternatively, they could choose for her to walk onto the blank canvas of the present, with minimal thought given to the past or future. Their final option is to allow her to return to the stone room in which she slept, until she feels ready to awaken. The choices that people make may reveal their readiness to engage in the therapeutic process and the degree to which they are able to do so, especially if they are invited to imagine themselves in Perdu's position.

There are no right or wrong choices to make – simply alternatives to explore. The story could be used in a single session or may be explored in more depth over several sessions. As well as the narrative, there is a mini script, which can be used as an additional resource. It has five potential characters: Perdu and the four enchanted doors, who each tell the story from their perspective.

The Lost One (narrative)[2]

Her clothes were in tatters, her bare feet bruised. She paced back and forth across the icy stone floor, aimless, lost in thought. She was lonely, her fine hair matted, her cheeks sunken and her eyes glazed. She knew that her name was Perdu, but could remember nothing more.

---
* The text of this story can be downloaded and printed at www.pavpub.com/find-your-way-resources

There were doors on all sides of the room she paced. Scared of what might be on the other side, she dared not see if they were unlocked. Hours passed by relentlessly, one day merging into the next. Night and day became indistinguishable. She lived yet did not feel alive. Hope had been vanquished. She did not know how long she had been within these walls and as time passed, her fear and fatigue intensified. She remained where she was, neither reaching for a door nor calling out for help.

The doors in the room were enchanted and often spoke to one another. She could not hear them. They watched over Perdu as she moved around the room or tried in vain to fall asleep. They grew increasingly concerned for her and one night, as she lay staring into the darkness, they decided that it was time to wake her fully. Each door led to a different realm and while they could not agree which she should enter first, they knew they must help her. So, together they rattled and creaked, then threw themselves open, flooding the room with sunlight.

Perdu was startled by the sound and blinked rapidly, struggling to adjust to the unfamiliar light. She felt a strong urge to close her weary eyes, to pretend that nothing had changed. She then froze in terror as she heard one of the doors speak, and saw that all four now stood wide open. Then something stirred deep within her – a faint desire to see what lay beyond her loneliness. She stood up slowly, her sense of anticipation increasing. Despite her fear, she followed her instincts and moved cautiously towards the first door.

She stood at the threshold and saw a flight of steps leading down to a pool of swirling water. The enchanted door spoke softly, its voice inviting, wise and familiar:

'Hello, Perdu. I am the door to the past. Walk carefully down the steps and enter the pool of water. You will remember who you are. You will see your past and although you cannot change it, you will no longer remain in the dark. There is much to discover, a myriad of joy and pain. Be careful though, as if you stay too long in my realm, you may find it difficult to leave.'

She took a step backward, feeling her throat and chest tighten. She then turned towards the second open door. Again, she stood at the threshold. A stairwell rose up before her, leading towards a cloud of colourful mist. The door spoke to her, its voice mysterious and alluring:

'Welcome, Perdu. I am the door to the future. Walk up the stairwell and into the mist. There you will discover a variety of potential futures. Explore the possibilities and you will see there is meaning to be found. You must remember, however, that the future is not static and while my world has much to offer, your future can only take its true shape when you are ready to step into the present.'

She felt confused, unsure what to do, so turned towards the third door. There were no stairs beyond this threshold, only a clear platform stretching out before her. In the distance she saw a bright light and the door then spoke, its voice bright and encouraging:

Story 2: The Lost One

'Greetings, Perdu. I am the door to the present. Walk over my threshold and you will step onto the blank canvas of today. Move towards the light and you will live in the moment, aware of your surroundings; the sounds, sights and aromas. You may enter this space with or without knowledge of the past and free of yearning for the future. Neither the past nor the future will define you.'

She felt a little more confident, life seeping back into her veins, but then hesitated. She turned away, following her desire to face the final door. She found herself staring at a mirror, in which she saw a room with an ice-cold stone floor, doors on every side, each one closed. The door spoke tenderly:

'There's no need to fear, Perdu; I know you are tired and confused by all you have seen. I am the door to Slumber. I offer no threshold for you to cross. I simply invite you to return to your slumber. You may remain in this room and we will continue to watch over you, until you feel ready to walk through a different door. Nothing will change until you choose it to.'

She sighed, uncertain which threshold to cross. She looked around the room, her eyes resting on each doorway, and spoke for the first time, her voice echoing around the room:

'I'm not sure what to do. I don't know which way to go. I would like things to change and I'm glad that I can now hear you. Yet I'm confused and afraid of getting lost again. Where should I begin?'

The story pauses here, with Perdu voicing her concerns, unsure what to do.

Imagine you are now in her place: Which doorway would you choose to walk through?

Whatever you decide, remember that nothing is static, even when it seems to be so.

The choice is yours.

Creative activities

Several activities can be offered in relation to *The Lost One* and new activities may also be created. The list below describes key exercises that have been used successfully with groups, and some can be adapted for individual work. You do not have to introduce every activity, nor follow the order in which they are listed. Discussion, however, is often an effective way to begin. The energy or nature of a group – or an individual's initial response to the story – will also guide you towards the most appropriate and effective way of working with it. Some people will find improvisation challenging, for example, and will prefer to engage in script work. On the other hand, you might have selected this story in order to steer your students or clients in a specific direction – to encourage self-reflection, for example. There is no right or wrong way to work with the story, just as there is no right or wrong choice for Perdu.

Discussion and choices

After sharing the story with the group, ask them to move into pairs or small groups and encourage them to discuss what they thought about the story, which door they think Perdu should move through and why they think this. If working with an individual, discuss this directly with them. It may help them to consider what door they would choose for themselves if they were faced with these choices, and you can also ask each person to select a line from the story that makes an impact on them. After these discussions, bring the group back together and invite everyone to share their thoughts. If the group is working in pairs, one approach is to ask each member to say what their partner decided and why. If working with an individual, adapt the process accordingly. It is also important to remember that the choices people make at this point may reflect something significant about their current mood and mental state, or their memories.

Dramatic tableaus

The four doors in *The Lost One* lead to different lands that are symbolic of varying states of mind or thought processes. Invite the members of your group to form mini groups based on which door they choose for Perdu to move through first: Past, Present, Future or Slumber. In these groups, participants can then work together to create a dramatic tableau (defined as a group of motionless figures representing a scene) to represent their chosen land. They can do this using their bodies. Voice can also be used to add words or sound effects. The tableaus can be either still or moving and if there is access to props, a selection of materials (different colours and textures) and percussive instruments could be useful. When ready, the groups should be encouraged to show one another their dramatic tableaus.

Artwork

As described in the exercise above, ask the members of your group to form mini groups based on which door they choose for Perdu to move through first: Past, Present, Future or Slumber. In these groups, participants can work together to create a piece of art or craft work to represent their land. They can do this using whatever arts, crafts and collage materials are available. When ready, the groups should be encouraged to present their creations to one another. Alternatively, your participants can produce individual pieces of artwork.

Creative writing

A helpful strategy to introduce creative writing is to ask an individual (or members of a group) to imagine what may lie in Perdu's past, what she might discover in her potential future or what she could find in the present. They can begin by selecting one of the four doors for Perdu to walk through, and then explore what happens next through creative writing. This could be written in either narrative or script form and works equally well with an individual or a group.

Improvisation

There are five characters to explore and bring to life through improvisation. Depending on the size of a group, participants could take turns to play the four enchanted doors, or they could form mini groups. Perdu could also be played by several people and

Story 2: The Lost One

may be either male or female. Parts of the mini script below could also be used. Props, costume and sound effects may be added to enhance the process. With an individual, roleplay with the facilitator is also effective.

The Lost One (mini-script)

There are five named parts in the following mini script. In a large group, participants could take turns to play the four enchanted doors (changing on each page, for example) or could form mini groups. Perdu could also be played by several people and may be either male or female. The script should be adapted accordingly and director, sound and design roles may be useful.

Door 1 (Voice of the Past):	Inviting, wise and familiar
Door 2 (Voice of the Future):	Mysterious and alluring
Door 3 (Voice of the Present):	Bright and encouraging
Door 4 (Voice of Slumber):	Kind, dreamy and gentle
Perdu (The Lost One):	Tired, confused, lost and alone

Setting:	*A room with four enchanted doors (props, costume and sound effects may be used). Suggested stage directions are shown in italics.*

Door 1:	Her clothes are in tatters.
Door 2:	Her bare feet are bruised.
Door 3:	She paces back and forth.
Door 4:	Aimless, lost in thought.
Door 1:	I think she's lonely.
Door 2:	I think she's confused.
Door 3:	She's forgotten who she is.
Door 4:	She's awake and yet asleep.
Door 1:	Her fine hair is matted.
Door 2:	Her cheeks are sunken.
Door 3:	Her eyes are glazed.
Door 4:	I'm not sure she can see the four of us?

Story 2: The Lost One

Door 1:	And yet we stand on each side of this room!
Door 2:	I think she sees us, though doesn't yet hear us.
Door 3:	She's never tried to open us.
Door 4:	She's scared of what might be on the other side.
Perdu:	One day merges into the next.
Door 1:	The hours pass by relentlessly.
Door 2:	Night and day are blurred.
Door 3:	She lives yet does not feel alive.
Door 4:	She has lost hope.
Perdu:	How long have I been here?
Door 1:	Her fear and fatigue have intensified.
Perdu:	I'm so tired, I just want to sleep.
Door 2:	So she remains, neither reaching for one of our handles nor calling out for help.
Perdu:	*(Lies down on a blanket and tries to sleep)*
Door 3:	I think she should enter the present.
Door 4:	What if she needs a little more sleep?
Door 1:	No, it's time for her to wake up, to understand her past and move forward.
Door 2:	I disagree; she should explore future possibilities and hope will awaken.
Door 3:	We simply need to help her?
Door 4:	Then perhaps we can gently wake her?
Door 1:	If we throw ourselves wide open, sunlight will flood the room.
Door 2:	Breaking the darkness!
Door 3:	Breaking the silence!
All Doors:	*(They rattle and creak, then throw themselves open and sunlight fills the room.)*
Perdu:	What's happening? *(Startled by the sound of the doors opening, she blinks in the unfamiliar light.)*

Story 2: The Lost One

Door 4:	She's awake!
Perdu:	Who's there? *(She stands up in fright – hearing the door speak for the first time.)*
Door 2:	She's scared!
Door 3:	I think she can hear us.
Door 4:	Can you hear us now?
Perdu:	Yes. *(She nods cautiously.)*
Door 1:	Don't be afraid, we've always been here.
Perdu:	*(She wants to close her weary eyes, to pretend that nothing has changed. Then something stirs deep within – a faint desire to see what lies beyond her loneliness. She moves cautiously towards Door 1, her sense of anticipation increasing.)*
Door 1:	Hello, Perdu. I am the door to the past. Stand at my threshold and you will see a flight of steps leading down to a swirling pool of water.
Perdu:	What should I do?
Door 1:	Walk carefully down the steps and enter the pool of water.
Perdu:	What will happen to me?
Door 1:	You will remember who you are. You will see your past and although you cannot change it, you will no longer remain in the dark.
Perdu:	I'm not sure I want to.
Door 1:	There is much to discover, a myriad of joy and pain. Be careful, though, as if you stay too long in my realm, you may find it difficult to leave.
Perdu:	*(She takes a step backwards, feeling her throat and chest tighten, then turns towards the second door.)*
Door 2:	Don't be frightened, Perdu. Come and stand at my threshold. I am the door to the future. You will see a stairwell rising before you, leading towards a cloud of colourful mist.
Perdu:	What must I do?
Door 2:	Walk up the stairwell and into the mist. There, you will discover a variety of potential futures. Explore the possibilities and you will see there is meaning to be found.
Perdu:	I'm not sure I can.

Door 2:	There's nothing to fear. You must simply remember that the future is not static and while my world has much to offer, your future can only take its true shape when you feel ready to step into the present.
Perdu:	*(She feels confused, unsure what to do, so turns slowly towards the third door.)*
Door 3:	Come closer, Perdu. There are no stairs beyond my threshold, only a clear platform stretching out before you, and in the distance a bright light.
Perdu:	What must I do?
Door 3:	Cross my threshold and you will step out of your slumber, onto the blank canvas of the present. Move towards the light and you will live in the moment, aware of your surroundings – the sounds, sights and aromas.
Perdu:	I'm not sure I can do it.
Door 3:	You may enter this space with or without knowledge of the past and free of yearning for the future. Neither the past nor the future will define you.
Perdu:	*(She feels a little more confident, life seeping back into her veins, though hesitates and turns away, intrigued to see what lies beyond the final door.)*
Door 4:	Come now, Perdu. I know that you're tired and may be confused by all you have seen. I am the door to slumber and I have no threshold for you to cross. I only have a mirror that reflects the room in which you now stand.
Perdu:	I don't understand.
Door 4:	I am inviting you to return to your slumber. You may remain in this room and we will continue to watch over you, until you feel ready to walk through a different door. Nothing will change until you choose it to.
Perdu:	*(She sighs, uncertain which threshold to cross, then voices her concerns.)* I'm not sure what to do. I don't know which way to go. I would like things to change and I'm glad that I can now hear you. Yet I'm confused and afraid of getting lost again. Where should I begin?

Examples of work in practice

You may discover that while some clients enjoy having a copy of the story to follow, others prefer to relax and listen. Likewise, some might respond well to script work and others will favour a freer, more spontaneous approach. As reflective discussions develop among one group, another will choose to remain in the creative realm. Choice is a prevailing factor here, just as in Perdu's story, where four doors open and options are given. It is imperative that everyone is heard and their choices are respected. In a group, this could prove challenging at times and as a facilitator, one should try to be as flexible as possible, while encouraging compromise and finding the most appropriate method with which to proceed. Three examples follow, in which pseudonyms are applied:

Waking Anna – a 19-year-old with PAWS

I began working on a specialist ward for women with eating disorders 18 months ago. The first client referred for 1:1 Dramatherapy sessions was Anna. She was 19 years old and acutely unwell. She remained on a nasogastric feeding tube for many months and her self-neglect was extreme. I was told that during her first few months on the ward, she had spoken very little and rarely left her bed. Towards the end of her long admission, the team agreed that PAWS (pervasive arousal withdrawal syndrome) was the most appropriate diagnosis for Anna: 'Young people with PAWS refuse to eat, drink, walk, talk or care for themselves in any way for several months or more. They completely withdraw socially, including from their family' (Ellern Mede, 2019).

When I arrived to see Anna for her third session, she was asleep in bed and appeared to have neither the inclination nor the energy to meet. I tentatively asked if she would like to hear a story instead and although her eyes remained closed, she nodded, adding a quiet 'yes'. I then sat by her bed and read her *The Lost One*. As I read, Anna gradually began to wake up, first opening her eyes, then sitting up in her bed. By the end of the story, she was alert, sitting on the edge of her bed, keen to discuss the meaning of the story and to explore the different choices offered to Perdu. The state of slumber was also discussed in relation to her regressed presentation on the ward during her first few months of admission. After reflecting on Perdu's choices, Anna decided that the door to the present seemed the best and safest place for her to begin.

Offering the story to Anna on this occasion seemed to break down unconscious barriers, enabling us to connect in a therapeutic (though perhaps unconventional) manner. Although the session took place by her bedside, moving forward she never missed a session and gradually felt able to meet outside of her room and eventually off the ward. Mirroring Perdu's awakening in the story, Anna had literally 'awakened' whilst listening to the tale. *The Lost One* had also introduced a symbolic language that she and I were able to refer to in future sessions.

Several months after first hearing the story, Anna asked if she could bring *The Lost One* to the Dramatherapy group on the ward, suggesting that her peers might like to hear it. The group then worked with the story together. This was a significant moment in her therapeutic journey. It showed that her confidence was clearly developing and that she felt ready to assimilate (and share) what she was learning in one-to-one therapy.

Exploring choices – young women with EUPD

Four young women on the specialist ward for EUPD – introduced in Chapter 1 – attended the Dramatherapy session in which *The Lost One* was first shared. They were aged between 18 and 22. Listening to the story led to a reflective discussion, during which each client expressed what they would do if faced with Perdu's choices. Pseudonyms are used.

1. **Sarah** (introduced in chapter 1) was feeling both tired and annoyed. She responded sensitively to the story, however, explaining that she felt she could relate to the character of Perdu. She said that she would choose to return to 'Slumber' at the end of the story, as she did not yet feel ready to walk through the door to the past, present or future.

   Interestingly, it was Sarah who had inspired the story of *The Lost One*. She loved princesses and unicorns, though struggled with oppressive depression and often described herself as 'stuck'. The original title of the story was *The Lost Princess*. Of the four clients who attended the session, Sarah was the most responsive.

2. **Ellie** was feeling very tired. Initially, she was not keen to listen the story. She did not know why, however, so changed her mind and agreed. During the discussion that followed the storytelling, she expressed clear opinions. This was unusual for Ellie, who often said 'I don't know' or 'I'm not sure' when asked for her opinion or thoughts during group sessions. She felt strongly that Perdu should enter the door to the past, so that she could learn who she was and everything about herself.

   This was poignant, as Ellie had endured sexual trauma that she had suppressed for a long time, and only began to speak about in therapy several months later. In this session, however, she felt sure that Perdu must confront her past in order to move forward, which suggests that Ellie's understanding of the therapeutic process of healing (and its necessity) was beginning to emerge, though perhaps unconsciously at this stage. When she was ready, however, she was able to apply to herself what she believed Perdu needed to do, and after a long admission she was successfully discharged home and continues to do well.

   Lara (introduced in chapter 1) was feeling low in mood. She responded thoughtfully to the story and said that if she was given the choice that Perdu was offered, she would enter the door to the future, as she liked neither her past nor her present. Lara was also very far from home, which she found incredibly difficult. She therefore had a short admission.

3. **Rachel** (introduced in chapter 1) had recently been diagnosed with ASD (autistic spectrum disorder) as well as having EUPD. She was feeling low in energy, and in response to the story reflected that she would be as confused as Perdu at the end, not knowing whether to enter the door to the past, present or future. It was as though Rachel remained in a state of 'slumber' throughout the session, waking just enough to relate to the story's protagonist, Perdu, who was likewise confused and struggling to 'awaken'. Rachel listened to the different responses from her peers, which may have given her hope that things could change and shift.

The Lost One has since been used with many individuals and groups on this ward. They seem to find this story easy to relate to and simple to follow, whatever their mood and mental state.

Themes arising – women with schizophrenia

Sharing *The Lost One* with clients on the female step-down unit (introduced in chapter 1) resulted in a mix of responses, some of which led to script and enactment work over several sessions. In general, this client group (who are predominantly diagnosed with psychotic disorders, including schizophrenia) have been very responsive to story work. Three examples follow, in which pseudonyms are used.

1. **Tina** was a client in her early 30s, with medication-resistant paranoid schizophrenia (mentioned in chapter 1). She thought that Perdu should enter the door to the past, as she would never be able to move on unless she faced her past. When working with either written stories and scripts, or spontaneous character and story-making, Tina was able to focus and express herself, her visual and auditory hallucinations temporarily abating.

2. **Bailey** was a client in her early 30s, with medication-resistant schizophrenia (mentioned in chapter 1). She was dedicated to the Dramatherapy group, though at times avoided participating in certain activities due to her spiritual beliefs and OCD. She had a very strong response to this story and although she took part in the story and script reading, she shared at the end that she had not liked *The Lost One*. She explained that she felt a very personal connection to Perdu, the protagonist, who she believed was experiencing severe OCD symptoms. Bailey shared that in the past she had experienced debilitating OCD that had prevented her from leaving her house, even her bedroom at times, for fear of touching the door handles. Her aversion to the story was acknowledged and she was reassured that she had done well to express her views and to share her personal experience.

3. **Raya**, a client in her late teens, had paranoid schizophrenia and was a dedicated member of the Dramatherapy group. Her level of engagement would fluctuate depending on her mood and the intensity of her psychotic symptoms. She responded positively to the story of *The Lost One* and particularly enjoyed participating in dramatic enactment, guided by the mini script.

It is interesting to note that OCD was not a theme I had consciously thought of when writing this story. Bailey's strong response to *The Lost One* was then a reminder of how powerful and evocative stories can be, in ways we may not expect. After Bailey shared how she felt about the story, the group was reminded that the stories were open to interpretation, with no clear endings, allowing individuals to connect with them on different levels and to discover their own meaning within them. As a facilitator, one must therefore remain vigilant when using symbolic stories, ready to work with any thoughts, feelings, associations, memories or themes that may arise.

References

Dickens C (1843) *A Christmas Carol. In Prose. Being a Ghost Story of Christmas.* London: Chapman & Hall.

Ellern Mede (2019) Treatment of Pervasive Arousal Withdrawal Syndrome. Available at: https://ellernmede.org/eating-disorders-information/pervasive-arousal-withdrawal-syndrome/

Gersie A (1997) *Reflections on Therapeutic Storymaking: The Use of Stories in Groups* (Kindle edition). London and Philadelphia: Jessica Kingsley Publishers.

Perrault C (1697) The sleeping beauty in the wood. In *Stories or Tales from Times Past, with Morals: Tales of Mother Goose.* Paris.

Schulz F (1790) *Rapunzel.* Based on the story *Persinette* (by Charlotte-Rose de Caumont de La Force, published in 1698) which was influenced by the Italian tale *Petrosinella* (by Giambattista Basile, published in 1634).

Story 3

Guardian of Dogs

Rejection, Abuse, Trust and Recovery

Illustration by Nicky Morris

Introduction

Significant themes are interwoven throughout *Guardian of Dogs*, subtly introduced through the five canine characters' substories. These include neglect, rejection, abuse, trust, abandonment, bereavement, fear, hope and recovery. While their stories offer powerful metaphors for human issues, the topic of animal cruelty and mistreatment is also evident and current, so may be considered and explored separately.

There are six main characters in the story: five are domestic dogs, whose lives have pushed them out of human society. In an ancient forest, they have come together as a pack and embarked upon a search for the Guardian of Dogs (the sixth character). She is a spirit dog who they are hoping can help them. As with all the stories in this collection, the journey has no clear ending and individuals can choose how the story develops or ends. Although the six dogs have been given gender types, this is not fixed and the words in the narrative (and mini script) could be changed accordingly and their names adjusted:

The Guardian of Dogs: A Siberian Husky. She is a spirit dog – ethereal, strong and wise. She is the protector of all dogs, able to answer their questions and grant requests.

This character was inspired by my clinical supervisor Kate McCormack's late dog, Tess – a Siberian Husky who became a PAT (Pets as Therapy) dog and visited many hospital wards with Kate. During supervision sessions, Tess would comfort me when I was feeling emotional or stuck for words and Kate explained that it was as though Tess always knew what people needed from her. She was beautiful, gentle, yet strong, and with her wolf-like appearance and ancient heritage, she was the perfect dog on which to base the Guardian of Dogs character.

Gray: A male greyhound and the leader of the pack. He is intelligent, kind and determined. Once a successful racing dog, he grew slower with age. No longer wanted by his human family, he was neglected and escaped to the forest to avoid being put to sleep (euthanised).

Research into the treatment of retired greyhounds supports this character's story (PETA, 2019a; ASPA, 2019), as does information on the greyhound breed (Dog Time, 2019a).

Steph: A female Staffordshire bull terrier. Bred to fight, she is feisty and tenacious. She was used by humans in illegal dog fights and, during a police raid, took the opportunity to escape. In the pack, she discovers there is more to her than aggression and mistrust.

Research into the underground world of dog fighting supports this character's story (Aid Animals, 2019), as does information about the Staffordshire bull terrier breed (Dog Time, 2019b).

Choux: A female chow chow (otherwise known as a chow). She is shy and cautious. Abandoned in the woods by her owners, she feels confused and rejected. She is slow to trust others and to believe that she is of any use to anyone.

Information about the chow chow breed supports this character's story (Dog Time, 2019c).

Ben: A young male beagle. He is excitable and sociable. Bred in an animal testing laboratory, he finally escapes after the humans he had trusted began to hurt him and one of his older brothers warned him to run away and never return. He loves the freedom of living outdoors, though longs for company.

This character's story is supported by research into scientific studies using animal testing, for which beagles are still bred. They remain the most popular choice for laboratories (PETA, 2019b; Top Dog Tips, 2018; BFP, 2019).

Peggie: A female pug. She is anxious, yet brave and affectionate. Grieving for her loving human, who died in their home, she is fearful of strangers, but had to leave her home in search of food and water.

Information about the pug breed supports this character's story (Dog Time, 2019d).

Guardian of Dogs (narrative)[3]

The pack slept soundly, the wind howling in the distance. Protected from the elements, they were huddled in the mouth of a cave near the ocean. They were an unusual ensemble, a mix of breeds, ranging in size and temperament. They had travelled through an ancient forest, followed the web of streams that led to a great river and finally reached the sea – a mysterious, glorious expanse of water.

The Guardian of Dogs watched them as they slept. She knew they had been searching for her. Not wishing to disturb them, she left without a sound. The pack were soon woken by the rattling snores of their smallest member, Peggie. They stretched and yawned. Before leaving the safety of the cave, they looked at one another, remembering how they had met and how their lives had changed.

Gray was proud and gentle, a mature greyhound and a natural leader. Once envied by his peers and adored by humans, his legs had grown tired and when he stopped winning races, his future became bleak. To escape the terror that lay before him, he had raced to the forest and began his search for the Guardian, a spirit dog he was told of as a puppy. He then found Ben, an excitable young beagle, who had escaped from an animal testing lab. He was enthusiastic yet naïve and Gray felt compelled to take care of him.

Together they had followed the stream and, while hunting a few days later, Gray witnessed a confrontation between two females: Peggie, an affectionate Pug, who was alone following the death of her human; and Steph, a feisty Staffordshire bull terrier, who had fled from a dog fighting den. Gray had approached them calmly, sensing they were strong yet vulnerable. Meanwhile, Ben found Choux, a large, fluffy chow chow, abandoned in the forest. They had all suffered in the human world, so Gray brought them together as a pack and told them of his quest.

---

* The text of this story can be downloaded and printed at www.pavpub.com/find-your-way-resources

Story 3: Guardian of Dogs

Their search for the Guardian was now almost at an end. They had faced many challenges and discovered hidden strengths. During their darkest moments, they had doubted her existence, though longed to believe the legendary stories they had heard. It was here, at the edge of the ocean, that she was said to live. The five dogs now stood as one entity, watching the sun rise grandly into the open sky, hoping for her arrival.

The Guardian of Dogs appeared suddenly before them, ethereal and majestic, her blue eyes gleaming. They knew it was her, a Siberian husky with a luxurious white and charcoal coat. She barked softly, asking them each to come closer and to share their stories with her.

Gray was the first to speak:

'I am Gray. I used to run like the wind and won so many races. Each time, I was showered with affection and praise. Sadly, when my legs began to tire, the humans who once cared for me began to neglect me. It felt as though my life was slipping away.'

The Guardian acknowledged his sorrow and he spoke on:

'Sensing danger ahead, I felt I must leave, so ran with the speed of my youth towards the forest. I knew that to survive, I had to reach the ocean, to find you, my beautiful Guardian.'

Gray's eyes filled with tears as he looked at her and thought of all he had experienced. Steph then moved boldly forwards and nuzzled him. She was grateful for his guidance and for accepting her into the pack, despite her quick temper and mistrust of anyone who crossed her path. She was strong-willed, with a lust for life:

'I'm Steph. I was bred to fight and believed no dog could be my friend. My human pack were confusing too; yelling at me one moment, hugging me the next, then ignoring me, as they drank and smoked together. One night, a pack of uniformed humans burst into the darkness that surrounded the pit where I had survived many fights. Members of my human pack shouted "police, run!" and I knew it was time to move on.'

The Guardian recognised her resentment and courage. Steph continued:

'I felt no sadness for the life I left behind and bounded towards the forest at the edge of town, certain no human would follow. I thought I must dominate every creature in the woods and was ready to kill if necessary. In the pack, I then discovered that my fighting skills could also help others and that I had the capacity to love and to be loved.'

She turned away, embarrassed by her emotions, then nudged a reluctant Choux forward:

'I once enjoyed time alone, relaxing in the shade of my garden, sauntering at my own pace. I was proud of my ancient heritage and loyal to my humans. The night they left me in a clearing in the woods, far from anywhere I recognised, I knew instinctively that I would never see them again.'

The Guardian sensed her despair and encouraged Choux to say more:

'I don't know what I did wrong and with a heavy heart, I curled up on the soft moss beside a nearby stream and closed my eyes. I felt unloved and with no reason to wake, I slept for many hours, perhaps days. When I first met Ben, I could not understand why he liked me. Gray then welcomed me into the pack and gradually I came to trust them and grew accustomed to Ben's affections.'

Choux shyly retreated and looked to Ben. From the moment he had first glimpsed her asleep by the stream, he had been besotted. Her yawn had revealed a unique blue-purple tongue and the lustrous mane of hair around her face was unlike that of any dog he had seen. Keen to share his story with the Guardian, he bounded forward, tail wagging, eyes bright:

'I'm Ben. I escaped from a lab and a fate I dare not imagine! I had thought myself lucky to live there, as the humans fed me well and I had canine friends to play with. I was happy until the humans I trusted began to hurt me. I didn't understand why. Then my older brother came to me, with swollen, bloodshot eyes. He told me to run to the forest and never return!'

The Guardian understood his disappointment and Ben continued:

'I followed his command and discovered the woods were incredible; the sounds, smells and, most of all, the space. I didn't enjoy being alone, though, and was keen to befriend any creature I met. This didn't always work out well, so I was glad when Gray took me under his wing. I love our pack and I'm worried what will happen now that we've reached the end of our journey.'

Sensing Ben's need for reassurance, Peggie trotted forward and licked his ear.

'I'm Peggie. My life was devastated when the human I loved collapsed and never woke up. I stayed hidden under his bed when strangers came to our house and took him away. Never again would I snuggle in his lap, hear his kind voice or sleep on his feet.'

The Guardian acknowledged her loss and Peggie said more:

'I didn't want to leave our cherished home, though, hungry and alone, I cautiously ventured into the woodland at the back of our garden. Afraid of strangers, I barked at every unfamiliar sound I heard and when I first met Steph, she terrified me! Then Gray encouraged us to join his quest to find you and on our journey, my spirits began to lift.'

The Guardian had listened to each of their stories intently. Moved by their courage, she understood both their losses and hopes. She barked softly again, asking them each to step forward, to ask whatever they needed to know and desired. The pack looked at one another, unsure where the next step of their journey would lead…

The story pauses here.

The next steps of the pack's journey are for you to discover and decide.

Creative activities

Guardian of Dogs is particularly helpful for group work, as the six characters that feature are of equal focus and a wide variety of themes can be explored. Several activities can be offered and new activities may also be created. Key exercises will be described, which have been used successfully with groups. Some can also be adapted for individual work. You do not have to introduce every activity, nor follow the order in which they are listed. Discussion, however, is often an effective way to begin. The energy or nature of a group – or an individual's initial response to the story – will also guide you toward the most appropriate and effective way of working with it. Some people will feel confident to participate in dramatic enactment, for example, while others will prefer to express themselves through creative art or writing. On the other hand, you might have selected the story in order to steer your students or clients in a specific direction – to improve communication skills, for example. There is no right or wrong way to proceed.

Discussion and choices

After sharing *Guardian of Dogs*, encourage your students or clients to discuss the story and to identify which of the dogs they feel most connected. Each person can also choose a line in the story (about their chosen dog, perhaps) that makes an impact on them. If there are more than six participants, splitting into pairs or smaller groups may be useful.

After these discussions, bring the group back together and invite everyone to share their thoughts. If working in pairs, one approach is to ask each member to say what their partner decided and why. If working with an individual, adapt the process accordingly. It is again important to remember that the choices people make at this point are likely to reflect something significant about their current mood and mental state, or memories.

The following questions will be helpful:

Two key questions to consider:

- To which member of the pack do you feel most connected?
- What might each dog ask (or request from) the Guardian of Dogs and how might she respond?

Further questions can include:

- What challenges might the dogs have faced on their journey together?
- Considering their personalities and past experiences, how might they have helped one another and in what ways do you think their journey may have changed them?

Questions of a more direct, personal nature may also be asked:

- Imagine that you are a dog, about to meet the Guardian of Dogs. What type of dog would you be (consider breed, physical description and personality traits, etc)?
- What question would you like to ask the Guardian?

Artwork

Your clients or students can use whatever arts, crafts and collage materials are available to engage in the following activities. This is equally effective for both individual and group work:

A. Invite your participant/s to create a piece of artwork (either 2D or 3D) to symbolise their chosen dog (either one of the story characters, or one they have imagined), adding the question that this dog would like to ask the Guardian of Dogs.

B. Alternatively, invite your participant/s to create a piece of art (either 2D or 3D) to represent either the Guardian of Dogs or how they would imagine their own personal Guardian to look. Again, they can add a question they may like to ask.

If working with a group, encourage your clients or students to show one another their artwork when ready, as sharing and witnessing each other's creations is an important part of the process.

Creative writing

A helpful strategy to introduce creative writing is to ask an individual (or members of a group) to imagine what would happen if the story were to continue. There are many possibilities. What would each of the dogs in the pack ask the Guardian of Dogs, for example, and what answers might she give? After this, would they remain as a pack, or separate and move in different directions? Alternatively, your clients or students could focus on the continuing journey of a single member of the pack, rather than write about the whole group. Their past experiences could also be explored further, or the questions offered earlier in the chapter could be used. Creative writing can be in either narrative or script form and works equally well with an individual or group.

Character work

Several groups have responded positively to *Guardian of Dogs*. It has a lot of scope for both character work and dramatic enactment through hot seating, roleplay and improvisation. Although six roles are indicated, characters can be shared, added or omitted, to adapt to each group's needs. The questions listed earlier could also be used as a starting point for improvisation.

Roleplay and hot seating (or interviewing) are techniques that help people to explore characters further – to identify their strengths, weaknesses, hopes and fears, etc. Hot seating involves each member of the group taking turns to imagine themselves in a chosen role, while their peers ask them questions. Roleplay, however, is a more fluid process, during which people may improvise a scene together in character.

The following activities could be offered:

1. Create a montage of mini scenes that focus on the memories that the dogs share in the narrative, describing their former lives with humans.
2. Create a montage of mini scenes that bring to life the various meetings between the dogs in the forest, as described in the narrative.

3. Improvise the scene that opens the story, with the five dogs waiting to meet the Guardian, hoping she will appear.
4. Continue the story from the moment the narrative ends, using improvisation to explore what each of the dogs ask the Guardian and the answers she offers.

A personalised version of the hot seating and improvisation process can also be used, which developed spontaneously in a session described later in this chapter.

Personalised character hot seating and improvisation:

For this activity, the Guardian could be played by either a participant or the facilitator. Members of the group choose a canine role by imagining themselves as a dog who has been through an experience that in some way mirrors their own life experience. They can choose the breed, name and personality type. Each of them is then interviewed by their peers, using a simple hot seating process. From this process, a group improvisation can develop, during which each new character approaches the Guardian of Dogs and asks for help in the form of a question, and the Guardian can answer them.

Guardian of Dogs (mini script)

The script below features the six characters and two scenes, introducing a more structured style of dramatic enactment. A third scene can also be created, either through improvisation or creative writing, or a combination of both. Participants could take turns to play different characters and, if working with a large group, smaller groups of six could form. There is also the potential for creative, non-acting roles, such as director and props/costume manager.

Guardian:	A Siberian husky. She is ethereal, strong and wise, the protector of dogs in need.
Gray:	A greyhound. He is the leader of the pack, intelligent, determined and kind.
Steph:	A Staffordshire bull terrier. She is a feisty survivor, tenacious and loyal.
Choux:	A chow chow. She is shy and cautious, having been abandoned by humans.
Ben:	A beagle. He is trusting, excitable and sociable, keen to be part of a pack.
Peggie:	A pug. She is anxious, yet brave and affectionate, grieving for her human.

Scene 1	*(The words in italics are suggested stage directions):*
Guardian:	The pack sleep soundly, the wind howling in the distance. Protected from the elements, they have huddled in the mouth of a cave, near the ocean. They have journeyed far to find me; through an ancient forest, along a web of streams that led to a great

	river and finally to the edge of the sea, this mysterious, glorious expanse of water.
Pack:	*(Asleep)*
Peggie:	*(Snores loudly – waking herself and the rest of the pack)*
Gray:	Good morning pack. Are you ready?
Ben:	I can't believe our search for the Guardian is almost over.
Steph:	During our darkest moments, we doubted her existence, Gray.
Peggie:	Though we longed to believe the legendary stories you told us.
Gray:	Don't worry, I understood your fears. I also felt afraid.
Ben:	And you heard the stories when you were a puppy, Gray?
Gray:	Yes.
Ben:	And it's here, at the edge of the ocean, she lives?
Gray:	Yes.
Choux:	Whatever happens, I'm grateful that you brought us together, Gray.
Ben:	Me too!
Gray:	Thank you.
Peggie:	We've grown so strong.
Steph:	We have, although after all we've been through, she had better exist!
Ben:	So, come on, Steph, let's find out.
Choux:	I'm not sure I'm ready to face my destiny.
Ben:	Don't worry, Choux. Just remember how we met and how things have changed.
Steph:	There's nothing to be afraid of. I can protect all of you.
Gray:	Relax, Steph. We won't need to fight. The Guardian is kind and wise. She will answer our questions and guide us.
Peggie:	I'm ready, Gray.
Ben:	Me too!
Pack:	*(They nod in agreement, leave the cave and follow Gray to the edge of the ocean)*
Gray:	Now we must stand together at the ocean's edge.

Story 3: Guardian of Dogs

Peggie:	As one entity.
Gray:	Yes.
Ben:	And we wait for her to arrive?
Steph:	That's right Ben, we wait.
Choux:	The sun is rising over the sea, it's so lovely.

Scene 2

Guardian:	*(She appears suddenly before them; ethereal and majestic – a Siberian husky with blue eyes and a thick coat of white and charcoal)*
Gray:	*(whispers)* It's her!
Ben:	*(whispers)* Her blue eyes are gleaming!
Peggie:	*(whispers)* Her coat's so luxurious!
Guardian:	*(She speaks softly)* Come closer, my friends – I know that you have travelled far and I can see that you are ready to share your stories with me.
Gray:	*(Steps forward – he is proud and gentle – a greyhound, respected by his pack)* I am Gray. I used to run like the wind and won so many races. Each time, I was showered with affection and praise. Sadly, when my legs began to tire, the humans who once cared for me began to neglect me. Other friends I knew from the racecourse mysteriously disappeared and it felt as though my life was slipping away.
Guardian:	I'm sorry, Gray.
Gray:	Sensing danger ahead, I ran with the speed of my youth towards the forest.
Guardian:	Why the forest?
Gray:	I knew that to survive, I must cross the ancient woodland to reach the ocean, where I would find you, my beautiful Guardian. *(Gray's eyes fill with tears as he looks at her and thinks of all he has experienced)*
Guardian:	And who are your brave friends?
Gray:	I met them in the forest. They too had suffered in the human world and knowing that they would also benefit from your guidance,

Story 3: Guardian of Dogs

	I brought them together as a pack. Travelling as a group has helped us to survive the journey here.
Steph:	*(Moves boldly forward – nuzzles Gray, grateful for his guidance and for accepting her into the pack. She's a strong-willed Staffordshire bull terrier)* I'm Steph. I was bred to fight and believed no dog or human could be my friend. Despite my quick temper and mistrust of anyone who crossed my path, Gray believed in me and invited me to join the pack.
Guardian:	And what of your life before you met them, Steph?
Steph:	My human pack were confusing, often violent. They would yell at me one moment, then hug me and later ignore me, as they drank and smoked together. One night, a pack of uniformed humans burst into the darkness that surrounded the pit where I had survived many fights. Members of my human pack shouted 'police, run!' and I knew it was time to move on.
Guardian:	So you went to the forest?
Steph:	Absolutely. I felt no sadness for the life I left behind and bounded towards the woodland at the edge of town, certain no human would follow. At first I thought I must dominate every creature there and was ready to kill if necessary.
Guardian:	Then something changed?
Steph:	Yes, in the pack I discovered that my fighting skills could also help others and that I had the capacity to love... *(she pauses, embarrassed)*
Gray:	... and to be loved, Steph.
Steph:	*(She nods shyly, backs away from the Guardian and nudges Choux forward)* Go on, Choux, it's your turn to speak.
Choux:	*(A large, fluffy chow chow – she speaks softly and carefully)* I am Choux. I once enjoyed time alone, relaxing in the shade of my garden, sauntering at my own pace. I felt proud to be a chow chow and I was loyal to my humans. The night they left me in a clearing in the woods, far from anywhere I recognised, I realised that I would never see them again and had no idea what I had done wrong.
Guardian:	I'm so sorry, Choux.

Choux:	With a heavy heart, I curled up on the soft moss beside a nearby stream and closed my eyes. I felt unloved and with no reason to wake, I slept for many hours, perhaps days.
Ben:	*(An excitable young beagle. Interrupts)* ... and I woke you with a lick!
Choux:	It's true – and when I first met Ben in the forest, I couldn't understand why he liked me. He introduced me to Gray, who welcomed me into the pack, and gradually I became used to them and grew accustomed to Ben's affections. *(She shyly retreats and looks to Ben, who is besotted with her)*
Ben:	*(He bounds forward – keen to share his story – tail wagging, eyes bright)* I'm Ben. I escaped from a lab and a terrible fate!
Choux:	Thank goodness.
Ben:	I enjoy being with both humans and dogs, so I'd thought myself lucky to live in the lab. I was well fed and had friends to play with.
Guardian:	So, when did you learn the truth, Ben?
Ben:	I was happy until the humans began to hurt me. I didn't understand why and then my older brother came to me one night – his eyes swollen and bloodshot. He told me that I must to run to the forest and never return. I could see the terror in his eyes, so followed his command.
Guardian:	And how did it feel to leave the lab?
Ben:	I was nervous at first and then discovered that the woods were incredible; the sounds, smells and most of all the space. I didn't enjoy being alone, though, and was keen to befriend any creature I met – which didn't always work out well!
Gray:	Luckily, I found him before he got into too much trouble.
Ben:	Yes, Gray has taught me so much and I love our pack. I'm just worried what will happen now, as we've reached the end of our journey.
Guardian:	I understand, Ben.
Peggie:	*(Sensing Ben's need for reassurance, she trots forward and licks his ear. She is a pug, the smallest in stature, anxious, yet brave and affectionate)* I'm Peggie and my life was devastated when the human I loved collapsed and never woke up. I stayed hidden under his bed when strangers came to our house and took him away.

Guardian:	I'm sorry for your loss, Peggie.
Peggie:	I knew that I would never again snuggle in his lap, hear his kind voice or sleep on his feet. Yet I didn't want to leave our cherished home.
Guardian:	So, what brought you to the forest?
Peggie:	I was hungry and thirsty, so cautiously ventured into the woodland at the back of my garden. Afraid of strangers, I barked at every unfamiliar sound I heard. I was terrified when I first met Steph.
Steph:	You were so brave, though, Peggie – small, yet feisty. I was impressed by the way you stood your ground.
Gray:	And I felt such respect for you both that day.
Peggie:	I will never forget it, Gray. You invited us to join you and although I was scared, I knew it was the right thing to do. The pack understood that I missed my human and travelling with them on this journey has somehow helped to lift my spirits.
Guardian:	Thank you, Peggie. I have listened carefully to all your stories and I feel moved by your courage. I understand both your losses and hopes. Step forward now, each of you, and ask whatever you want to know and desire.
Pack:	*(They look at one another, unsure where the next step of their journey will lead)*

Scene 3

The final scene is for your group to improvise or devise a script, as the next step of the pack's journey is for them to discover and decide. (They may want to refer to the questions asked at the end of the narrative.)

Examples of work in practice

This section includes a description of various activities that developed with two of the groups that have worked with this story. Individual responses are also shared. The story work continued with both groups over several weeks. One group was based on a low secure ward for women with a diagnosis of EUPD (emotionally unstable personality disorder) and the other in a rehabilitation service for women with a range of mental health difficulties, primarily EUPD and schizophrenia.

Connections – *young women with EUPD*

The canine characters in *Guardian of Dogs* (or at least aspects of them) were inspired by several clients I met on a ward offering specialist treatment for women with EUPD (described in chapter 1): Choux, Peggie, Ben and Steph in particular. A small group of young women attended the sessions that focused on the story. Each of them had a primary diagnosis of EUPD. Many of them were very fond of dogs, a few missed their own dogs and all of them found it easy to connect emotionally to at least one of the dogs in the story. Some of their responses are described below and pseudonyms are used.

1. **Lara** (mentioned in chapter 2) attended two sessions that focused on the story. She responded positively when first hearing it and offered to read the part of Ben, the excitable young Beagle, in the narrative. Following a discussion in small groups, however, she shared that the character she felt most connected to was Steph, the Staffordshire bull terrier, who learns that it is possible to trust again despite being treated badly in the past. In the second session, the mini script was introduced and she chose to read the part of the Guardian.

2. **Mary** (introduced in chapter 1) attended the first session in which the story was shared. She said initially that she was feeling terrible, but managed to engage in every activity and responded positively to the new story. She agreed to read the part of Gray, the wise and gentle leader of the pack, in the narrative. Following a discussion in small groups, however, she also reflected that the character with whom she felt most connected was Steph, the Staffordshire bull terrier, because she showed that change was possible.

   Although Mary's group attendance fluctuated throughout her admission, whenever she came to a session she connected deeply to the process and often expressed herself more freely than others. This was particularly evident in her response to story work.

3. **Rachel** (mentioned in chapters 1 and 2) attended the first session in which the story was shared. She said initially that she was feeling anxious and agitated. Despite this, she managed to engage in every activity and responded thoughtfully to the new story. She offered to read the part of Peggie, the bereaved Pug. Following a discussion in small groups, she said that she felt an emotional connection to both Peggie and Choux (the abandoned chow chow) because she enjoyed being alone and felt unsure of herself. At the end of the group, Rachel reflected that, although she still felt anxious and agitated, she was pleased to have come.

   It is interesting to note that Rachel (who was diagnosed with both EUPD and ASD) participated more actively than usual in this session, which may have partly been due to her love of dogs and all animals, with whom she felt more comfortable than people.

4. **Sarah** (mentioned in chapters 1 and 2) attended two sessions that focused on the story. At the start of the first session, she shared that she was feeling extremely tired and was in the process of trying different medications to help to improve her sleep. She appeared to be more subdued than usual, though managed to engage fully in every activity and responded thoughtfully to the new story. Sarah offered to read the part of Steph, the Staffordshire bull terrier, in the narrative. Following a discussion in small groups, she explained that Steph was the character with whom she felt most connected, as she was misunderstood – as many Staffies are. She also said that like Steph, although she was initially scared to trust others, she had learnt that there were individuals she can trust and who will treat her well.

During the second session, Sarah again felt very tired, though made the effort to participate fully. The mini script was introduced and she chose to read the role of Steph. She did so with expression, though at the end of the session she said she felt even more tired.

It is interesting to note that Sarah was often very flat in affect (with an apparent absence of emotional response, her voice and face showing little expression). Whenever she read from a narrative or mini script, however, this shifted considerably, as though she 'came to life'.

5. **Tracey** (introduced in chapter 1) attended the first session in which the story was shared. She said initially that she was feeling quite good and engaged fully in every activity. She responded thoughtfully to the new story explored and, following a discussion in small groups, reflected that the character with whom she felt most connected was Choux, the dog abandoned in the forest by her owners with no idea why. Tracey explained to the larger group that she was able to relate to Choux's story from a personal perspective, having also been 'dumped' as a baby and not knowing why. Her revelation took courage and the end of the session she said she was still feeling good and had enjoyed the group, despite the emotional connection she had made with the character of Choux.

6. Both **Amy** and **Darla** (introduced in chapter 1) missed the first session, in which the story was shared, but attended the second session, when the mini script was introduced. They responded very differently to the process: Amy embraced the opportunity to participate, choosing to take on the role of Gray, the wise and peaceful leader of the pack; Darla, on the other hand, felt agitated and anxious throughout the session. She chose not to actively participate and later explained that she found any type of written activity stressful, as it reminded her of being at school.

Women in a mental health step-down unit

The women I work with in a therapeutic step-down service (described in chapter 1) have a range of mental health difficulties. In the Dramatherapy group, we explored *Guardian of Dogs* over several weeks, through various activities, discussions and script work. During one session I shared the background research I had done into the mistreatment of various dog breeds, which seemed to help this group to connect to the story and find meaning within it. Some of their responses are described below. Pseudonyms are used.

1. **Katy** was a committed member of the group. She was in her early 20s, diagnosed with EUPD and mild learning disabilities. The week we were due to explore *Guardian of Dogs*, she was waiting to be transferred to an acute ward, having become violent. Feeling anxious and irritable, she initially refused to attend, but changed her mind and decided to try, as she particularly enjoyed story and script work. After listening to *Guardian of Dogs*, she said that she felt a strong connection to the character of Steph, who finds it difficult to trust anyone and has a temper due to the difficult life she has led. She then played this role and created her own (similar) character for the hot seating exercise.

2. **Tina** (mentioned in chapter 2) was diagnosed with medication-resistant paranoid schizophrenia. She responded with enthusiasm to *Guardian of Dogs* and used her expressive acting skills to bring several roles to life when reading the narrative. Despite responding to psychotic symptoms throughout the session, she managed to focus enough to participate and shared that she found the story very poignant, especially after hearing more about the mistreatment of various dog breeds.

3. **Raya** (mentioned in chapter 2) was in her late teens, diagnosed with paranoid schizophrenia. Her mood and symptoms fluctuated significantly each week. Despite this, she remained a consistent group member. During the session that explored *Guardian of Dogs* through improvisation, Raya was feeling relatively stable and her mood was bright. She responded thoughtfully to the story and said that she liked the mysterious quality of the Guardian.

A hot seating exercise developed in this session, which involved each participant imagining themselves to be a dog with personality traits that matched their own or that had been through a similar life experience. They chose the breed, name and age, then each of them was interviewed by their peers and the facilitator, using a simple interview process. From this activity a group improvisation then emerged, during which each new character approached the Guardian of Dogs and asked for help in the form of a question. Raya was keen to play the role of the Guardian and during the activity she responded sensitively to the other characters (played by her peers), offering them positive advice and reassurance. This revealed a development in her self-confidence and capacity to understand and empathise with others. Raya, Katy, Tina and their peers found this final activity particularly empowering.

References

Aid Animals (2019) Dog Fighting. Available at: https://aidanimals.com/animal-cruelty/dog-fighting/

ASPA – American Society for the Prevention of Cruelty to Animals (2019) Greyhound Racing. Available at: https://www.aspca.org/animal-cruelty/other-animal-issues/greyhound-racing

BFP – Beagle Freedom Project (2019) FAQ. Available at: https://bfp.org/faq/

Dog Time (2019a) More About This Breed, in 'Greyhound'. Available at: https://dogtime.com/dog-breeds/greyhound#/slide/1

Dog Time (2019b) More About This Breed, in 'Staffordshire Bull Terrier'. Available at: https://dogtime.com/dog-breeds/staffordshire-bull-terrier#/slide/1

Dog Time (2019c) More About This Breed, in 'Chow Chow'. Available at: https://dogtime.com/dog-breeds/chow-chow#/slide/1

Dog Time (2019d) More About This Breed, in 'Pug'. Available at: https://dogtime.com/dog-breeds/pug#/slide/1

PETA – People for the Ethical Treatment of Animals (2019a) Greyhound Racing: Death in the Fast Lane. Available at: https://www.peta.org/issues/animals-in-entertainment/animals-used-entertainment-factsheets/greyhound-racing-death-fast-lane/

PETA – People for the Ethical Treatment of Animals (2019b) Dogs in Laboratories. Available at: https://www.peta.org/issues/animals-used-for-experimentation/dogs-laboratories/

Top Dog Tips (2018) A Timeline of How and Why Beagles Were Used in Lab Experiments. Available at: https://topdogtips.com/beagles-used-in-lab-experiments/

Story 4

Boy in a Tree

Avoidance, Self-Preservation, Fear and Courage

Illustration by Nicky Morris

Introduction

Boy in a Tree was inspired by my teenage nephew, who has ASD (autistic spectrum disorder) and feels most at ease when sitting high in the branches of a tree. At times he chooses to sleep through the day and remains awake at night, to avoid the many things he does not understand and finds challenging. There are many people who feel overwhelmed by day-to-day life and would at times prefer to avoid it. In relation to this, *Boy in a Tree* explores themes of avoidance, self-preservation, relationships, communication, adolescence, fear and courage.

Boy in a Tree works well with groups and can be very useful for individual work, as there is a single protagonist, rather than several. Following the story, creative activities are suggested, one of which begins by inviting participants to imagine that they are crouching on a branch at the top of a tree, where they must consider who they are and what they would prefer to avoid. This exercise can quickly shift the work into a more personal dimension, while maintaining the safety and containment of dramatic metaphor.

At the end of this chapter, English teacher Dom Roy reveals the potential of using *Boy in a Tree* (and other stories of this style) with boys in a secondary school: inspiring them to develop their creative writing skills, while also helping them to understand their own emotions and psychological processes. He also describes the specific relevance of this story to teenage boys with ASD (autistic spectrum disorder). As dramatherapists Lewis and Banerjee reveal, therapeutic stories can benefit the emotional, psychological and social development of young people with autism (2013).

Boy in a Tree (narrative)[4]

The boy sat quietly at the top of an oak tree. He felt safe there, crouching like a cat, high above all that scared him. Each day, his mother would visit, urging him to come down, and although her efforts felt futile she refused to give up hope. She often told him that change was possible and things might not be as bad as they seemed.

At nightfall, he would ease himself down the strong trunk that kept him rooted to the earth. He felt more relaxed when the world was sleeping – free from people, their confusing words and expectations. As the sun began to rise, he would return to his branch. He focused simply on survival and enjoyed the company of the squirrel who shared his leafy home. Together, they watched children play, saw lovers embrace and observed teenagers muddle their way through life. At times, the boy felt an urge to join them. Yet he remained where he was, avoiding the pressure of having to understand things that made little sense to him.

One morning, when the sky was particularly bright, he woke to the loud coos of a dove and was astonished to see a girl sitting at the top of a cedar tree in the distance. As she studied the world below, he wondered who she was and why she was there. The dove perched beside him and, sensing she wanted to tell him something, he looked into her eyes and listened.

---

* The text of this story can be downloaded and printed at www.pavpub.com/find-your-way-resources

'I can take a message to her', she cooed.

The boy felt uncertain. His stomach began to churn and his mouth grew dry. Abruptly, he turned away from the dove and tried to get back to sleep.

As dusk approached, he awoke to a crimson-streaked sky. Instinctively, he looked towards the cedar tree. The girl was no longer there and he felt an unfamiliar yearning. Then he saw her, singing softly among the bluebells at the foot of a nearby birch tree.

'You should climb down and meet her', cooed the dove.

'You might like her', suggested the squirrel.

The boy froze; his mind felt blank. He turned away from them, imploring them to let him sleep. He waited until darkness swamped the forest, then slid stealthily down the trunk and went in search of berries, roots and fresh water. As he washed his pale face and drank thirstily from a stream, he was startled by the sound of splashing. He looked downstream and saw the girl from the tree, paddling. He wanted to speak to her, though words evaded him and he feared they may never come. Afraid she might see him, he hurried back to the oak tree.

At sunrise, the dove began to coo insistently. Woken by her call, the boy cleared his bleary eyes and was astonished to see a group of people circling the girl's tree. Some of them were shouting, their voices angry, possibly desperate. Others called to her in softer tones. He saw that she was distressed. She clung to the trunk of her tree, visibly trembling, her face hidden. The dove settled on his shoulder.

'Go to her', the dove cooed.

'She needs you', added the squirrel.

He knew the girl was in trouble and he wanted to help, but didn't move, as he too felt frightened. The animals encouraged him further.

'You can do it, boy', cooed the dove.

'You are braver than you know', said the squirrel.

His muscles tensed, his breathing accelerated. Then he slid skilfully down the trunk and ran towards the unknown. Stopping close to the cedar tree, he cried out to the group,

'Leave her alone!'

They turned to face him and the sound of his heartbeat thundered in his ears.

'She's not ready to come down', he said.

'So, what do we do?' they asked. 'It's been so long.'

The boy thought for a moment, then shared his mother's words:

'Tell her that change is possible and that things may not be as bad as they seem.'

'We just want her to be with us', they explained.

'Then give her time', he replied.

They looked at one other and, in quiet agreement, dispersed.

The boy looked up at the girl and shyly asked if she was okay. She smiled and thanked him, then turned away, embarrassed. In a daze, he ambled towards the bluebells surrounding the birch tree. He heard the dove's song above and, gazing upwards, he was surprised to see a child high in the branches. His eyes then followed the flight of the dove and he was astounded to see many people of different ages, both male and female, sitting in the uppermost branches of other trees in the forest. All of them were crouched like cats, looking at the world below. The boy was confused, wondering why they were there. The dove flew by him and cooed:

'You are not alone, boy.'

'People take to the trees for many reasons', added the squirrel.

The boy stood quietly among the bluebells, then looked back at the girl. The sun had risen and he was unsure what to do. Should he try to speak to her again? Perhaps he could greet his mother in daylight? Or maybe he should simply return to the branch of his trusted oak tree and wait to see what the next day might bring?

> The story pauses here and the boy in the tree has choices before him,
> as do the girl and all the others taking refuge in the forest. The next step of their
> journey is for you to decide.

Creative activities

In response to *Boy in a Tree*, many paths can be explored through discussion, then ideas and characters can be developed through improvisation, creative writing, role play and script work, etc. New activities may also be created. Key exercises will be described, which have been used successfully with groups. Some can also be adapted for individual work. You do not have to introduce every activity, nor follow the order in which they are listed. Discussion, however, is often an effective way to begin. The energy or nature of a group – or an individual's initial response to the story – will also guide you toward the most appropriate and effective way of working with it. Some people enjoy participating in script work, for example, while others may prefer the freedom of improvisation. On the other hand, you might have selected this story in order to steer your students or clients in a specific direction – to encourage creative writing, for example. There is no right or wrong way to work with the story, just as there is no right or wrong choice for the boy in the tree.

Discussion and choices

After sharing *Boy in a Tree*, encourage your students or clients to discuss what they thought about the story and to decide what they think the boy should do next. Each person can also choose a line in the story that makes the most impact on them. The following options may be considered:

- Should the boy return to the girl's tree and try to speak to her again?
- Should the boy wait for his mother to arrive (as she does every morning) and greet her on the land, in daylight?
- Should the boy try to speak to any of the people he now sees are also taking refuge in the trees?
- Should the boy return to the branch of his trusted oak tree and wait to see what the next day will bring?
- Where do you go (or take refuge) when you need time alone?

If there are more than six participants, splitting into pairs or smaller groups may be useful. After these discussions, bring the group back together and invite everyone to share their thoughts. If working in pairs, one approach is to ask each member to say what their partner decided and why. If working with an individual, adapt the process accordingly.

Create your own character

Imagine that you are crouching on a branch at the top of a tree and consider the questions listed below. They can be asked in the form of suggestions, while clients or students listen and reflect. Alternatively, they can be asked through the hot seating process, which involves each member of the group taking turns to imagine themselves in a chosen role, while their peers (or the facilitator) asks them questions.

- Are you human or animal?
- Are you an adult, teenager or child?
- Are you male or female?
- Why are you in a tree?
- What or who would you prefer to avoid?

Participants can also share their answers through a short monologue, story or script (as mentioned in the following 'Creative Writing' section). It is also important to remember that the choices and ideas expressed through this activity are likely to reflect something significant about a person's current mood and mental state, or memories.

Creative writing

There are several helpful strategies which can be used to introduce creative writing inspired by *Boy in a Tree*:

▶ Ask an individual (or members of a group) to imagine what would happen if the story were to continue. There are several possibilities, some of which were listed under the discussion heading. Participants could then continue to write either the narrative version of the story or the mini script that follows.

▶ Another option is for individuals to create a new story about the girl in the tree, or one of the other people taking refuge in the trees.

▶ Alternatively, participants might prefer to write a story about a character that they have imagined, based on the 'Create Your Own Character' activity described in the previous section.

Creative writing can be in either narrative or script form and works equally well with an individual or group.

Artwork

Invite your clients of students to create a piece of artwork, using whatever art and craft materials are available.

1. Ask them to consider where they would choose to take refuge if in need of time alone. They may have already explored this during the 'Discussion and Choices' activity. They can then create a piece of artwork (2D or 3D) to represent their chosen place.

2. Alternatively, they could create a piece of artwork (2D or 3D) to symbolise their favourite character, significant theme or chosen moment from the story.

If working with a group, encourage your clients or students to show one another their artwork when ready, as sharing and witnessing each other's creations is an important part of the process. This activity is appropriate for both group and individual work.

Boy in a Tree (mini script)

The following mini script may be used as a structured form of dramatic enactment, or a catalyst for further exploration of the story. It includes seven short scenes and features five characters (plus extras). An eighth scene could also be created, either through improvisation or with creative writing, or via a combination of both.

Participants could take turns to play different characters, or if working with a large group, smaller groups of five or more could form. There is also the potential for creative, non-acting roles, such as director, props/costume manager, etc.

Mother: Loving, persistent, yet weary

Boy: Anxious and stubborn, yet resourceful and kind

Squirrel:	Inquisitive, friendly and persuasive
Girl:	Withdrawn and gentle
Dove:	Wise and encouraging
Extras:	The children, adults and teenagers on the land; the crowd who gather around the trunk of the girl's tree and the other people crouched in the branches of trees across the forest.

Scene 1	Dove, Mother and Boy
Dove:	The boy sits quietly at the top of the oak tree. He feels safe there, crouching like a cat, high above all that scares him. His mother visits every day.
Mother:	Come down today, please?
Boy:	I can't.
Mother:	Change is possible, my love. Things might not be as bad as they seem.
Boy:	I'll come down at night – when the world is sleeping and free from people.
Mother:	It's such a beautiful day, though; maybe we could go for a walk?
Boy:	*(Shouts)* No. Just leave me alone. Let me sleep.
Mother:	Okay, I'm sorry. I understand… but I'll never give up. *(She walks away sadly)*

Scene 2	Squirrel, Boy and Extras
Squirrel:	Hello, boy.
Boy:	Hello.
Squirrel:	What are you doing?
Boy:	Nothing.
Squirrel:	Can you see the children playing?
Extras:	*(Play a ball game together)*
Boy:	Yes.
Squirrel:	Do you see the lovers embrace?
Extras:	*(Hug or hold hands)*

Story 4: Boy in a Tree

Boy:	I do.
Squirrel:	Can you see the teenagers muddling their way through life?
Extras:	*(Laugh together)*
Boy:	Yes, I see them.
Squirrel:	Don't you ever feel the urge to join them?
Boy:	Sometimes.
Squirrel:	Yet you remain in this tree?
Boy:	Yes.
Squirrel:	Why?
Boy:	Things make sense up here. I just want to survive, that's all. *(He tries to sleep)*
Scene 3	Girl, Dove, Squirrel and Boy
Girl:	*(Sits high on the branch of a cedar tree)* I'm safe here. No one can reach me.
Dove:	*(Perched on a branch near the boy, coos loudly to wake him)* Coo! Coo!
Girl:	No one can see me.
Squirrel:	Wake up, boy!
Girl:	No one can pressure me.
Dove:	Coo! Coo!
Boy:	*(Wakes up)* What is it, dove? What do you want?
Squirrel:	There's a girl at the top of the cedar tree!
Boy:	Who is she?
Squirrel:	I've not seen her before.
Dove:	I can take her a message for you.
Boy:	Why?
Dove:	She might need a friend.
Boy:	Not me.
Squirrel:	Why not, boy?
Boy:	My stomach's churning, my mouth is dry. Go away, please, let me

sleep. *(He lays back down on his branch and tries to sleep)*

Scene 4	Boy, Squirrel, Dove and Girl
Boy:	*(Wakes and sees the girl is no longer in the tree)* She's gone. Where is she?
Squirrel:	There, under the birch tree, among the bluebells.
Dove:	Listen!
Girl:	*(Hums softly)*
Squirrel:	You should climb down and meet her.
Boy:	Why?
Dove:	She might like you?
Boy:	I'm fine where I am.
Squirrel:	You might like her?
Boy:	My mind is blank. Go away, both of you.
Dove:	Darkness sweeps the forest now.
Squirrel:	You're safe.
Boy:	Okay. I'm going down.
Squirrel:	To find berries and roots?
Boy:	Yes.
Squirrel:	And water?
Boy:	Yes. *(Eases himself down the tree trunk and searches for berries and roots to eat. Then heads to the stream, drinks thirstily and washes his face)*
Girl:	*(Splashing further upstream – humming softly to herself)*
Boy:	*(Hears the humming, then sees her)* I want to speak, but the words won't come. *(Runs back to the oak tree)*
Scene 5	Dove, Boy, Squirrel, Girl and Extras
Dove:	*(Persistent, urgent tone)* Coo, Coo, Coo!
Boy:	*(Abruptly wakes)* What's the matter?
Squirrel:	Look over there, it's the girl in the cedar tree!

Story 4: Boy in a Tree

Boy:	*(Sees a group of people circling the girl's tree)* What's happening?
Girl:	*(Distressed, clinging to the trunk of her tree, visibly trembling, her face hidden)* Go away. Please. I like it here. Leave me alone.
Dove:	Go to her, boy.
Squirrel:	She needs you.
Boy:	I want to, but I can't.
Dove:	You're braver than you know.
Squirrel:	You can do it.
Boy:	*(Climbs down, muscles tense, heart pounding, and runs towards the girl's tree)*
Extras:	*(Shouting to the girl)* Get down now! You've been up there long enough!
	Come on, just climb down and join us!
Boy:	*(Shouts)* Leave her alone.
Extras:	*(Turn to face the boy)* Why?
Boy:	She's not ready.
Extras:	So, what do we do? It's been so long.
Boy:	Tell her that change is possible and that things may not be as bad as they seem.
Extras:	We just want her to be with us.
Boy:	Then give her time.
Extras:	*(Look at one other and in quiet agreement, disperse)*
Boy:	*(Looks up at the girl)* Are you okay?
Girl:	I think so.
Boy:	That's good.
Girl:	Thank you *(Turns away, embarrassed)*
Scene 6	Boy, Squirrel, Dove (and Extras)
Boy:	*(Walks towards the bluebells surrounding the birch tree)*
Dove:	*(Perches besides him)* Look up, boy.
Squirrel:	*(Sits the other side of him)* Do you see the child high in the

	branches?
Boy:	Yes!
Dove:	Now expand your vision!
Boy:	*(He looks across the many treetops and is astounded to see people of different ages, both male and female, sitting in the uppermost branches of other trees)*
Squirrel:	Do you see them all?
Boy:	I do.
Dove:	Men, women, boys and girls, all crouched like cats, looking at the world below.
Boy:	I see them, but I don't understand?
Squirrel:	You're not alone, boy.
Dove:	People take to the trees for many reasons.
Scene 7	Mother and Boy
Mother:	*(Quietly watching her son)* The sun has risen, and my boy stands among the bluebells. He doesn't know what to think or where to go. Will he go back to the girl in the cedar tree? Perhaps he'll wait for me to arrive? Or maybe he'll simply return to the branch of his trusted oak tree and wait to see what tomorrow brings?
Scene 8	*What happens next?*

Examples of work in practice

You may discover that while some clients enjoy having a copy of the story to follow, others prefer to relax and listen. Likewise, some might respond well to script work and others will favour a freer, more spontaneous approach. As reflective discussions develop among one group, another will choose to remain in the creative realm. Choice is the prevailing element here and it's imperative that everyone is heard and their choices respected. In a group, this could prove challenging at times, and as a facilitator one should try to be as flexible as possible, while encouraging compromise and finding the most appropriate method with which to proceed.

Hiding from the world – *Catia and Charlotte*

I initially wrote *Boy in a Tree* to help me to connect to Rachel (mentioned in chapters 1–3), who I met on the ward for women with EUPD. She had recently been diagnosed with ASD (autistic spectrum disorder) as well as having EUPD. She was 19 years old and found it very difficult to socialise with her peers and to express herself. Although she often self-isolated and her group attendance fluctuated, she responded well to the new stories I was writing. While themes of feeling misunderstood and choosing to hide away from the world are pertinent to Rachel and others with ASD (like my nephew), they also relate to people in different situations, faced with a variety of issues. As the Squirrel says to the boy, towards the end of the story: 'People take to the trees for many reasons.' This story has been introduced to many groups, as well as to several individuals engaging in 1:1 work. Two particularly poignant examples (using pseudonyms) follow:

1. **Catia** was in her early 20s. She was diagnosed with medication-resistant paranoid schizophrenia and struggled much of the time with intense paranoia and distressing hallucinations. We met on a secure step-down unit for women with a range of mental health difficulties (described in chapter 1). Catia was one of two young women who attended a session in which *Boy in a Tree* was shared. She rarely felt able to come to the group (or any sessions offered on the unit) due to how scared and upset she often felt. Mostly, she would remain in her bedroom, her safe space, frequently shouting and crying. On this day, however, she managed to attend and responded to the story with enthusiasm. She was able to focus throughout the session and was keen to engage in script work and dramatic enactment. She chose to play the role of the boy, which she did with sensitivity and honesty. At the end of the session, she said that she felt a deep connection to both the boy and the girl in the story. She explained that she understood what it was like to feel overwhelmed by life and to need to take refuge in a safe place, away from other people.

2. **Charlotte** was a young woman with anorexia nervosa, restrictive type. She was 20 years old and we met on a specialist eating disorder ward. During her first few weeks on the ward, she was keen to try out as many groups as possible, as she felt motivated to recover and wanted to see what might help her. During her first one-to-one Dramatherapy session, she was offered a choice of three stories to explore and she selected *Boy in a Tree*. We read it out together, alternating between paragraphs, then explored some of the questions found in the 'Discussion and Choices' section. Charlotte was fascinated by the story and how she was able to relate it to herself, her eating disorder and the dynamics within her family. We also read through scenes 1 and 2 from the mini script. Interestingly, although she felt a strong connection to the character of the boy, she chose to read the role of the mother in scene 1 and that of the squirrel in scene 2. She explained that she wanted to gain insight into another perspective, to see how it might feel to be the mother, father or friend of someone who is struggling and choosing to hide away from the world. Charlotte admitted that this was how she often felt. She also expressed her surprise at how closely the dialogue between the characters reminded her of conversations she had had with her own parents. She asked if she could show the story and script to her mother and was given a copy to keep. She also said that she now looked forward to reading more of the stories in future sessions.

Teenage boys in a secondary school (written by Dom Roy)

My name is Dom Roy and I have been a full-time teacher of English at a variety of schools over my 23-year career. The schools that I have worked at have included fully comprehensive state schools, an all girls' school, a private boys' school and an EBD unit for boys who cannot attend mainstream education, and I am currently Head of Year at Watford Grammar School for Boys. I have worked as a Head of English at two schools and I have also been a pastoral leader in two schools. I first read Nicky's stories earlier this year, while devising a scheme of work on the short story form to complement the school's new 'well-being' curriculum. I taught *Boy in a Tree* to two classes: a mixed ability class of Year 7 boys and a class of more challenging Year 9 boys. I also subsequently taught *Little Blue* to the Year 7 class, as I felt that the themes were so important to explore with the world as it is today. My reflections on this story are included in chapter 5.

Boy in a Tree was an immediate hit with both classes. The writing style was simple and the boys were able to fully engage with the story. Many students in the Year 7 class felt sympathy for the boy in the tree; some admired him for staying in the tree. The Year 7 class has an usually high number of boys with autism for a mainstream school and one of the ASD students wanted to read the story over and over again, as he felt that the boy in the tree was a version of himself. He immediately identified with the protagonist. The Year 7 students were initially frustrated by the ending as it did not lead to a definitive conclusion; however, after a period of paired discussion and reflection, most of them worked out that the story was about choices and how difficult they can be to make. I gave the Year 7 boys a variety of subsequent classroom activities to choose, so that they could explore the stories further. Most students chose to write paired scripts involving further interactions with the girl and the animals. The mini scripts that were produced by many, involved the boy in the tree finding a way down from the tree because he finally had a reason to leave. A few scripts introduced new characters that linked with the short story, but all the scripts did have endings that felt quite final. The Year 9 boys who chose to write continuation scripts were able to create more ambiguity and the endings were on the whole darker than those produced by the Year 7 boys.

The students who chose to continue the story in prose form were able to emulate the same economy of style in the writing, and these did not all have closure. In fact, one story ended with a cliffhanger, as the branch that the boy had clambered onto was close to breaking point and was just about to snap. The ASD students were curiously more inclined to have open-ended stories, after the class discussion about the way the story was about choice and how choices do not always lead to final resolutions. In the final analysis, nearly all the boys enjoyed the reading of the story and it made them verbally reflect on both the character's feelings as well as their own. Some even began to open up about the places they go to when they feel stressed.

References

Lewis J & Banerjee S (2013) An Investigation of the Therapeutic Potential of Stories in Dramatherapy with Young People with Autistic Spectrum Disorder. *Dramatherapy* **35** (1) 29–42.

Roy D (2019) *Emailed Report*. Consent given to include the report in this chapter.

Story 5

Little Blue

Immigration, Expectations, Relationships and Prejudice

Illustration by Nicky Morris

Introduction

Little Blue introduces several themes, which are gently explored: immigration, family expectations, relationships, prejudice and betrayal. The protagonist of the tale is Kororā (the Māori name for the Little Blue penguin). She is a Little Blue penguin, the smallest breed in the world and the only ones to have blue and white feathers. The story begins with her birth and childhood, then moves to her first day of hunting in the ocean and a secret friendship that develops with Dapper, a Black-Footed penguin from the native colony on the other side of the beach.

At the beginning of *Little Blue*, we learn that Kororā's parents and ancestors had travelled across the Indian Ocean to make a new home on the South African coast. Her colony are then overjoyed as she is the first chick to be born there. I initially wrote this story to try to connect to a young woman with EUPD whose parents had moved from Asia to the UK before she was born. She felt overwhelmed by the high expectations placed upon her. In the story of *Little Blue*, although Kororā appears to have a loving family, as she grows older she begins to feel confined by their expectations and struggles with the pressure she feels.

Other significant themes enter the story, such as the prejudice that people from different cultures or countries encounter (or might feel towards one another) and how this may be inherited, yet also challenged, by the younger generation. For example, both Kororā and Dapper have been warned to mix only with their own breed, due to fear and mistrust of others. This sadly remains a relevant issue in modern society, where it is often the newest immigrants who are most harshly judged or used as scapegoats. For example, psychological predictors of xenophobia have been linked to the unexpected result of the 2016 Brexit referendum, in which 52% of the UK public voted to leave the European Union (Golek De Zavala *et al*, 2017, p1). Anti-immigrant prejudice has been revealed as a major influence on the Brexit result and one 'pro-leave' poster was compared to Nazi propaganda (Johnston, 2017). The police also reported that the number of hate crimes against immigrants tripled following the Brexit result (Johnston, 2017). As Golek De Zavala *et al* explain, the 'Leave' campaign emphasised anxiety over immigration and the need to take firmer control over the UK's borders (2017). They suggest that 'Understanding whether prejudice motivated the Brexit vote or the Brexit vote legitimized and increased prejudice may be of lesser importance than understanding that individual predictors of prejudice are related to political choices that undermine diversity and harmonious intergroup relations' (2017, p12).

From a personal perspective, while writing *Little Blue*, I had not consciously thought about my own connection to its themes. My great grandparents were Polish immigrants, who changed their surnames to help them to assimilate into British society. I also have family in other parts of the world, some of whom originally fled from pogroms (the organised massacres of ethnic groups, specifically Jews, that began in the late 19th century across Russia and Eastern Europe) and others who survived the Holocaust (the mass slaughter of European Jews in Nazi concentration camps during the Second World War). Working in mental health settings, I also have many colleagues who have emigrated from Africa, the Caribbean and Eastern Europe. At times they are confronted by racial abuse, sometimes from service users who are very unwell. *Little Blue* is a story through which issues of racism and prejudice (usually born from ignorance and fear) can be addressed with any group, including staff and service users in hospital settings.

Finally, while Kororā's story offers a metaphor for human challenges, issues and relationships, information about the Little Blue and Black-Footed penguin breeds was also considered. This included conservation concerns, habitats, developmental stages and behaviours. It is understood, for example, that Little Blue chicks usually fledge at eight weeks and become independent, though remain very close to where they were raised and never move away (New Zealand Penguins, 2019). Another example is the factors contributing to the decline in the Black-Footed penguin population, which include a reduction in their food supply due to commercial fishing and oil pollution from tankers (Denver Zoo, 2019).

Little Blue (narrative)[5]

Kororā was the first of her kind born on the South African coast, or rather the first to survive. Her tiny community were delighted with her arrival and celebrated as the sun set, their hopes for survival revived. Her ancestors had travelled across the Indian Ocean, far from their homeland, in search of a new and better life. Many had died during the perilous journey, some trapped in giant fishing nets, others suffocated by oil spillage. Close to the beach where they finally settled, ferocious storms had drowned several brave travellers, while others were carried to safety. Her parents were among the survivors and although they were very young at the time, the memories had ingrained themselves, like a recurring nightmare. All the survivors were desperate to prolong their blood line, in memory of those they had lost.

As a tiny chick, Kororā was oblivious of her colony's desires. In awe of her surroundings, she simply felt loved. Her parents and extended family protected her and taught her all she needed to know about the culture and history of the Little Blue penguin, the delicate breed to which she belonged. She grew into a spirited young bird and at eight weeks old she left the comfort of her parents' burrow and joined the hunters at the edge of the ocean. She swam fast and free, her blue and white feathers glistening – gliding through the water with natural expertise. Diving beneath the waves, she met a young male penguin, larger than her, with a sleek black and white coat. They swam in unison, laughing together and sharing the shoals of tiny fish that flowed their way. His voice was loud and bold, his name Dapper. At dusk, they parted ways. He swam towards the far end of the beach, where the large trees loomed, and Kororā dug her own burrow and rested, while the land predators stalked the earth. The two met in the ocean times several times after this, though kept their friendship secret, having both been warned to mix only with their own kind.

As she continued to grow, Kororā began to understand the hopes bestowed upon her and felt stifled by her colony's efforts to protect her from the outside world. They

---

* The text of this story can be downloaded and printed at www.pavpub.com/find-your-way-resources

Story 5: Little Blue

expected her to be a perfect Little Blue and despite the birth of other chicks she was the first, so the burden remained. Shielded from many things, she began to grow restless and was keen to forge her own path. When fishing boats began to crowd the waters near their side of the beach, her community grew anxious and gathered to discuss their options. Kororā suggested that they ask the Black-Footed penguins for help – a large colony living among the trees on the far side of the beach. The others disagreed, fearful of change and adamant that the two species should remain separate. Kororā was frustrated. She thought of Dapper and knew there was nothing to fear. If she could find him and explain the difficulties they faced, she was sure that he and his Black-Footed family would agree to help. This was her opportunity to make a genuine difference and to unite the two breeds.

In the early hours of the morning, Kororā left the safety of her burrow and waddled towards the far end of the beach for the first time. The sun had not yet risen and although she feared the darkness, her desire for change gave her courage. After walking some distance, she saw a small group of Black-Footed youngsters coming towards her. Her excitement rose and then rapidly turned to fear when she saw their wings were flapping aggressively, their beaks raised.

'Vagrant!' one shouted.

'You don't belong here', squawked another.

'You're not welcome, Little Blue', spat the largest.

The angry group surrounded her and Kororā trembled where she stood.

'This beach belongs to us', another added.

'Go back to where you came from', they threatened.

Shocked and confused by their insults, Kororā stammered,

'I'm a penguin, just like you. I was born on this beach.'

'You're nothing like us', one barked.

'Just look at yourself', laughed another.

They continued to taunt her with their loud braying voices, then, seeing her eyes fill with tears, they turned away, laughing as they waddled to the ocean's edge. Kororā froze, desperate to run, yet rooted to the ground. It was then that she saw Dapper, standing awkwardly just a little further up the beach. He neither looked at her nor moved towards her and in that moment the reality of his betrayal sank in. He had seen everything yet done nothing.

Kororā's tears silently flowed and a young sea turtle, watching from beneath his shell, moved slowly towards her.

'Don't cry, little penguin', he said.

'They hate me and I've no idea why', she answered.

'You're different to them, that's all', he replied.

'I don't understand', she said.

'You're a Little Blue penguin, the smallest species in the world, the only ones with blue and white feathers', explained the sea turtle.

'Why does that matter?' Kororā asked.

'The Black Footed penguins are native to this land. They are fearful of difference and your family travelled here from afar', he replied.

Kororā shook her head in disbelief and looked sadly towards Dapper, who remained motionless, his head bowed.

'It makes no sense to me', she said.

'So, what will you do, Little Blue?' he asked.

'I don't know', she sighed.

'Nothing is as it should be. What can I do? My friend has lost his courage and abandoned me; the Black-Footed penguins have threatened me, and my community overprotect me, while pressuring me to be perfect. I know that I want things to change, though I've no idea where to start.'

Kororā's story pauses here and the ending is for you to explore.

Should she confront Dapper and ask him why he did nothing to help her?

Perhaps she should try to convince the Black-Footed gang to accept her?

Maybe she should abandon her mission to bring the two communities together, return to her colony and become the perfect Little Blue they want her to be?

The choice is yours.

Creative activities

There are many themes to unearth in the story of *Little Blue*, which can be explored through discussion, creative writing, improvisation, script work, etc. The following activities have been used successfully with groups and several have been adapted for individual work. You do not have to introduce every activity, nor follow the order in which they are listed. Discussion and guided questions, however, are often an effective way to begin. New activities may also be created. Remember that there is no right or wrong way

Discussion and choices

After sharing the story with a group, ask them to move into pairs or small groups and encourage them to discuss what they thought about the story and to consider what they would like to happen next. If working with an individual, adapt the process accordingly. It may help them to reflect on what they would do if faced with Kororā's predicament. The following questions will be helpful:

1. Should Kororā confront Dapper and ask him why he watched and did nothing while she was taunted by the Black-Footed penguin gang?
2. How might Dapper be feeling, having witnessed the incident between Kororā and the Black-Footed penguin gang? Why do you think he did nothing to help?
3. Should Kororā forgive Dapper?
4. Should Kororā challenge the group who taunted her and convince them to accept her?
5. Why do you think the Black-Footed penguin gang behaved how they did towards Kororā?
6. Should Kororā abandon the idea of forming an alliance between the two communities, return to her colony and become the perfect Little Blue penguin they want her to be?
7. Does Kororā have any other options?

After these discussions, bring the group back together and invite everyone to share their thoughts. You can also ask each person to identify the moment or line from the story that makes the most impact on them. If working in pairs, one approach is to ask each member to say what their partner decided and why. It's also important to remember that the choices people make at this point may reflect something significant about their current mood and mental state, or their memories.

Creative writing

A helpful strategy to introduce creative writing is to ask an individual (or members of a group) to imagine what would happen if Kororā's story were to continue. There are several possibilities and it may be helpful to refer to the questions asked in the previous section. Participants could continue to write the narrative version of the story, create a mini script or write a monologue for a chosen character: Kororā, Dapper or a member of the Black-Footed gang, for example. This activity works equally well with an individual or a group.

Artwork

Invite your clients of students to create a piece of artwork, using whatever art and craft materials are available. They can symbolise either their chosen moment from the story or the theme they connect with. If working with a group, encourage your clients or students to show one another their artwork when ready, as sharing and witnessing each other's creations is an important part of the process.

Dramatic enactment

There are several characters to explore and bring to life through dramatic enactment. This could take the form of hot seating, roleplay, improvisation or tableau work. Kororā is the central role, supported by her parents and members of the Little Blue community. Other characters are Dapper, the Black-Footed gang and the Sea Turtle.

▶ Create a tableau of your chosen moment

Ask your students or clients to identify the moment in the story that made the most impact on them. Invite them to dramatise their chosen moment in tableau form, using their peers to represent the characters included. Stepping into the role of director can be an empowering experience. It allows a person to take a step back from their own drama and encourages them to develop a new perspective. They could also choose a line from the narrative to add to their tableau.

▶ Roleplay and improvisation

Depending on the size of a group, participants could take turns to play the various characters, or they could form mini groups. Kororā, Dapper and the other roles might be played by several people and may be either male or female. With an individual, roleplay with the facilitator can also be effective. As described in chapter 3, roleplay and hot seating are techniques that aid character development, helping to identify what motivates them, their strengths, weaknesses, hopes and fears, etc. Hot seating involves each member of the group taking turns to imagine themselves in a chosen role, while their peers ask them questions. Roleplay, however, is a more fluid process, during which people may improvise a scene together in character – either a scene from the story or an imagined scene that takes place outside of the original narrative. Examples include:

1. Roleplay a scene between Kororā and Dapper that takes place after the original narrative ends. At this point, Kororā has realised that Dapper witnessed her clash with the Black-Footed gang and did nothing to help her.

2. Roleplay a scene between Kororā and her parents, during which they tell her about her ancestors' perilous journey across the ocean to create a new home for the next generation. In this scene, they may also tell her that she should mix only with her own breed, to protect herself and the community.

3. Roleplay a scene between Dapper and his parents or friends, during which they tell him he must only mix with his own breed, warning him to keep his distance from the immigrant penguins on the other side of the beach.

Little Blue (tableau sequence)

The sequence of dramatic tableaus presented below includes key moments from the story. Dramatic tableaus can be silent and still, or simple words, sounds and movement may be added. Narrator lines and dialogue can be improvised, devised or taken from the narrative to accompany the tableaus (examples are included below). Extra tableaus can also be formed. Props, costume and sound effects may be used to enhance the process and again, a director role could be helpful.

Tableau 1	**Celebrating Kororā's Birth** *(improvise dialogue, or use the following words):*
Narrator:	Kororā was the first Little Blue penguin born on the South African coast. Her parents and community were delighted and celebrated as the sun set.
Mother:	Welcome to the world, little one.
Father:	You're going to make us so proud.
Mother:	You're very special, Kororā.
Father:	You're the first chick to survive on this side of the beach.
Tableau 2	**Kororā's Independence** *(improvise dialogue, or use the following words):*
Narrator:	Kororā grew into a spirited young bird and at eight weeks old she left her parents' burrow and joined the hunters at the edge of the ocean.
Father:	It's time to leave us, Kororā.
Mother:	You must dig your own burrow now, darling.
Father:	And hunt for your own fish.
Kororā:	I'll make you proud, I promise. *(Kororā leaves her parents and stands at the edge of the ocean, ready to swim and hunt for the first time).*
Tableau 3	**Kororā and Dapper Meet in the Ocean** *(improvise dialogue, or use following words):*
Narrator:	Diving beneath the waves for the first time, Kororā met Dapper, a young male penguin, with a sleek black and white coat. They swam in unison, sharing shoals of tiny fish. They kept their friendship secret, however, as they had been warned to mix only with their own kind.

Dapper:	Hi. I'm Dapper.
Kororā:	Hello.
Dapper:	I've never seen a blue penguin before.
Kororā:	My name's Kororā.
Dapper:	I'm not supposed to mix with other breeds.
Kororā:	Me neither.
Dapper:	Would you like to swim with me?
Kororā:	I think so… come on… let's go!
Tableau 4	**Kororā's Mission** *(improvise dialogue, or use the following words):*
Narrator:	Kororā decided to travel to the other side of the beach to ask Dapper and the Black-Footed Penguins for help. When she arrived, however, she was confronted by an angry gang.
Gang 1:	Vagrant!
Gang 2:	You don't belong here.
Gang 3:	You're not welcome, Little Blue.
Gang 1:	This beach belongs to us.
Gang 2:	Go back to where you came from.
Kororā:	I'm a penguin, just like you. I was born on this beach.
Gang 3:	You're nothing like us.
Gang 1:	Just look at yourself.
Gang 2:	You're pathetic.
Kororā:	*(Begins to cry)*
Gang:	*(Laugh at Kororā and leave her to cry).*
Tableau 5	**Kororā and the Sea Turtle** *(improvise dialogue, or use the following words):*
Narrator:	Kororā was shocked and upset. She then saw Dapper, standing awkwardly, a little further up the beach. He neither looked at her nor moved towards her and in that moment the reality of his betrayal sank in. He had seen everything yet done nothing. Whilst she stood alone, crying, a sea turtle approached her.

Sea Turtle:	Don't cry little penguin.
Kororā:	They hate me and I've no idea why.
Sea Turtle:	You're different to them, that's all.
Kororā:	I don't understand.
Sea Turtle:	You're a Little Blue penguin, the smallest species in the world, the only ones with blue and white feathers.
Kororā:	Why does that matter?
Sea Turtle:	The Black-Footed penguins are native to this land. They are fearful of difference and your family travelled here from afar.
Kororā:	It still makes no sense to me.
Sea Turtle:	So, what will you do, Little Blue?
Kororā:	I don't know … nothing is as it should be. What can I do? My friend has lost his courage and abandoned me; the Black-Footed penguins have threatened me, and my community overprotect me, while pressuring me to be perfect. I know that I want things to change, though I've no idea where to start.
Tableau 6	**Kororā's Choice** *(This is an improvised scene or tableau, showing what the group choose for Kororā to do next. There could be several versions of this, which small groups could create, and the questions shared under the 'Questions and Choices' heading might be useful to consider).*

Examples of work in practice

Little Blue has been used with several client groups. You may discover that while some people enjoy having a copy of the story to follow, others prefer to relax and listen. Likewise, some might respond well to script work and others will favour a freer, more spontaneous approach. As reflective discussions develop among one group, another will choose to remain in the creative realm. Choice is the prevailing element here, just as in *Little Blue*, where Kororā has different options and must decide what to do next. It is imperative that everyone is heard and their choices respected. In a group this could prove challenging at times, and as a facilitator one should try to be as flexible as possible, while encouraging compromise and finding the most appropriate method with which to proceed. Poignant examples follow, in which pseudonyms are used:

Energising improvisation – *Katrina and Tamara*

Both women were in their mid-30s and regular members of the weekly Dramatherapy group on a secure step-down unit (described in chapter 1):

Katrina was diagnosed with bipolar disorder and was recovering from drug-induced psychosis. She was intelligent and creative, with a talent for both art and writing. Her mood and energy were often very low, however, and she struggled with suicidal thoughts.

Tamara was diagnosed with schizophrenia. She was often cheerful, though frustrated at times, and usually struggled to stay awake during sessions due to possible narcolepsy.

Both women responded positively to Kororā's story and enjoyed bringing the first two scenes of the tableau sequence to life. They improvised their own dialogue and movement, while I took the role of narrator, introducing each scene and adding sound effects and simple props. Katrina and Tamara laughed a lot during the session, especially when they dramatised the scene in which Dapper and Kororā first meet. They were unusually energised and alert, both sharing at the end that they had found the process very freeing.

Chosen moments – young women with EUPD

Little Blue was explored on a low secure ward for women diagnosed with EUPD (described in chapter 1). A group of clients responded with enthusiasm to the story and it was explored over several sessions. Initially, I told the group the story; after this, themes and characters were explored. In another session, artwork was created to symbolise chosen moments and in a final session, the tableau sequence was brought to life. Examples follow, using pseudonyms.

1. **Ellie** (mentioned in chapter 2) was the young woman who initially inspired this story. Her parents had moved from China to the UK before she was born and she felt overwhelmed by the high expectations placed upon her. She continuously battled against suicidal thoughts and strong urges to self-harm. Continuing the story work that began the previous week, the group selected characters and Ellie chose to be Kororā, the central figure. From a selection of key moments offered, she chose the joyful moment when Kororā first meets Dapper. During the enactment that followed, Ellie appeared unusually energised and connected. She and the student dramatherapist, Izabela, interacted via movement and improvised dialogue.

   Many months later, Ellie was preparing for discharge from the ward and we had two 1:1 sessions. I decided to tell her that she had inspired the story *Little Blue* and we read it again together. Ellie shared that she had been bullied in school for being Chinese. She was feeling both fearful and excited about being discharged and was pleased to keep a copy of the story.

2. **Tracey** (mentioned in chapter 3) was often avoidant of the Dramatherapy group, finding that it stirred too many memories and emotions. She was also apprehensive about story work, especially if it involved reading out loud, as she had dyslexia. She responded well to *Little Blue*, however, and in the third session she chose to portray the Sea Turtle, a wise character who offers support and advice to Kororā. Tracey felt a connection to the role and chose to use the script rather than improvise. At the end of the session, she reflected that she had challenged herself and achieved a great deal: reading a script out loud, maintaining direct eye contact and holding her

hand very close to the therapist's hand during the dramatic enactment of her chosen scene. Her efforts were acknowledged, together with the many contributions she had made to directing the other tableaus and scenes created by her peers.

3. **Darla** (mentioned in chapter 3) lacked confidence with reading. Darla was focused on getting well, so she could return to her daughter and become the mother she wanted to be. She responded with interest to the story *Little Blue* and connected to the moment when Kororā first dives into the ocean and hunts with her peers. The emotion she related to this was 'pride'. In the next session, participants were invited to create a piece of artwork inspired by their chosen moment and Darla drew a picture of Kororā, standing proudly at the ocean's edge, ready to dive in and swim for the first time. Her peers expressed appreciation of her work and she said she was pleased with it. Her drawing was simple yet powerful, perhaps symbolising her hope that with her forthcoming discharge she could start afresh and make a better life for herself and her daughter.

4. Amy and Anya both felt a strong connection to the moment of Kororā's birth.

    Anya (mentioned in chapter 1) explained that she was the first girl to be born in her family, after several decades of boys. At the end of the session she reflected that she had enjoyed the process, though had perhaps overidentified with an element of the story. During a supportive 1:1 session that followed, she explained that she was feeling guilty, thinking about how happy her parents had felt when she was first born, compared to how much they now worry about her and fear losing her.

    Amy (mentioned in chapter 3) had endured a very difficult childhood, complicated by medical problems. Her mother developed postnatal depression and her father was an alcoholic, who at one stage attempted to commit suicide. Amy said that she wanted to imagine being Kororā, newly born, her parents and community overjoyed at her arrival. This was perhaps the opposite of what she had experienced as a baby and bringing the moment to life through dramatic enactment made her feel very happy. She played the role of Kororā and was surrounded by her peers, who represented her parents and members of the colony, joyfully celebrating her arrival.

Personal connections – *Anna and Karly*

I worked with Anna and Karly on a specialist eating disorder ward for women (first mentioned in chapter 2). I saw them both for 1:1 Dramatherapy sessions and they also attended several Dramatherapy groups together. Both responded with interest and enthusiasm to the story and related closely to different aspects of it.

Karly was in her early 40s and had been recently diagnosed with anorexia nervosa, restrictive type. She was struggling to come to terms with the breakup of her 20-year marriage and had two children in their early 20s. In response to the story, she shared that Dapper's betrayal reminded her of how her husband had shocked and betrayed her, choosing to walk away from their marriage and now living with another woman.

Anna (described in chapter 2) was 20 years old and diagnosed with PAWS (pervasive arousal withdrawal syndrome). She felt a strong connection to the story for very different reasons to Karly. She had spent several summers on the beach in the country of her late mother's birth, where she had witnessed extreme tension and divide between many of the black and white citizens.

Teenage boys in a secondary school *(written by Dom Roy)*

My name is Dom Roy and I have been a full-time teacher of English at a variety of schools over my 23-year career. Before teaching the short story *Little Blue*, I introduced my class of 28 Year 7 boys to the idea of literature in context. We discussed the ways in which stories and literary texts are influenced by the era in which the stories were first written. Thus, the concept of a social, historical and political context to any written, visual or spoken text was explored. I gave the students five minutes in pairs to think about the things that were going on in society today that could be alluded to in the short story that we were about to read. I explained that the short story was written very recently and therefore the boys should think of recent events. The boys came up with the following: Trump and his behaviour, Brexit, knife crime, gangs and gangsters (which always comes up with boys) and global warming, among other things.

While the students did not specifically discuss immigration, as we read through the story there were mutterings of 'aaahh … it's about immigration and Brexit'. The boys immediately understood the story's message and by and large sympathised with Kororā's plight. They described her treatment as 'unfair' and 'unkind' in class discussion after reading the story and the vast majority of students sympathised with the treatment of the minority 'blue penguins' in their new land. There was a lone voice from a student who insisted that the same 'colours' would be better off being together as they would have the same morals. However, this view was immediately challenged by the rest of the class, who expressed the attitude that if they did not mix, then they would not understand each other.

The short story was successful in that it sparked some fierce debate and the relevant themes perfectly complemented the whole school theme for this half term, which is that of kindness.

References

Denver Zoo (2019) African Black Footed Penguin. Available at: https://www.denverzoo.org/animals/african-black-footed-penguin/

Golek De Zavala A, Guerra R & Simao C (2017) 'The Relationship between the Brexit Vote and Individual Predictors of Prejudice: Collective Narcissism, Right Wing Authoritarianism, Social Dominance Orientation'. *Frontiers in Psychology: Personality and Social Psychology.* Available at: http://www.frontiersin.org/people/u/485224

Johnston I (2017) Brexit: Anti-immigrant prejudice major factor in deciding vote, study finds people who met EU citizens living in Britain tended to have a good experience and were therefore more likely to vote Remain. *Independent.* Available at: https://www.independent.co.uk/news/uk/politics/brexit-racism-immigrant-prejudice-major-factor-leave-vote-win-study-a7801676.html

New Zealand Penguins (2019) Blue Penguin. Available at: http://penguin.net.nz/species/blue

Roy D (2019) *Emailed Report.* Consent given to include the report in this chapter.

Story 6

The Glass Wall

Confinement and Freedom, Attachment and Separation

Illustration by Nicky Morris

Story 6: The Glass Wall

Introduction

The Glass Wall presents the story of Fidget, a young sea otter confined to a glass enclosure in an aquarium. He craves freedom, yet in captivity he also experiences two positive relationships: with Jenna, a shy young woman who regularly visits him, and Lyla, an older sea otter and his surrogate mother. Fidget's story explores themes of attachment and separation, freedom and confinement.

The quest for freedom is a theme that often resounds in the hospital settings where I work, particularly on the step-down unit (introduced in chapter 1). As I wrote in my first book: 'Their cry for freedom resonates at different levels. Often voiced as a desire to leave the unit, to be taken off section or released from the mental health system, it also symbolises a deeper wish to be free from the intense emotions, paranoia, frightening hallucinations or flash backs, with which they struggle' (Morris, 2018, p114). While many service users feel physically restricted due to living on a ward or unit, some are legally confined by a mental health act section. Most also feel imprisoned by debilitating symptoms or the burden of traumatic memories. In my first book, freedom was also revealed as one of the five recurring themes in Dramatherapy sessions on the secure ward for women with EUPD (introduced in chapter 1):

'Freedom is a theme that continuously arises and may be explored from both a philosophical and practical perspective. It is a concept used to describe various qualities or states of being: the power or right to act, speak, or think freely; the state of being free (neither imprisoned nor enslaved) and the state of not being affected by something undesirable (Oxford English Dictionary, 2012, p287). I facilitate sessions in a relaxed manner, where choice is paramount. Most of the service users are on section and many have been abused throughout their lives. They feel disempowered by these experiences, so having choice throughout every session, motivates them to participate and helps to improve confidence and self-esteem. Although clients are often desperate to be taken off section and discharged from hospital, this is frequently complicated by their fear of how they will cope in the outside world. Their containment offers a degree of safety.' (Morris, 2018, p77)

Attachment and separation are also significant themes and relevant to most people. We form attachments throughout our lives, some healthy, others less so. Either way, separation can be challenging – both letting go and moving forward. How do we know when we – or they – are ready? Consider the parent and child relationship, for example, or the client and therapist relationship. How does a client or student move on from an institution that has been a safe place for them, even if they did not like it?

Finally, elements of the story were inspired by a visit to an aquarium where I witnessed a penguin in a glass enclosure repeatedly bang its head against the wall while under water. When I placed my hands against the glass, the penguin relaxed, and as I moved my hands along the wall it followed. When I was leaving, however, the headbanging routine began again and it was very difficult to walk away. I later read more about the aquarium and the incredible work they do towards conservation and rehabilitation. Their sea otter program, for example, was established in the 1980s to promote the recovery of the threatened southern sea otter population. As well as their research in the wild, they also treat and release injured otters they have rescued, and raise and release stranded pups through a surrogate programme, and also find homes for sea otters that can't return to the wild. Fidget and Lyla's characters were based on two of the sea otter programme's inhabitants.

The Glass Wall (narrative)[6]

They had stared into one another's eyes many times, yet this moment was distinctly different. He looked up at her, wide-eyed, and she knelt before him, tenderly stroking his soft coat for the first time. Jenna knew that she could do something that would genuinely change Fidget's life and yet she was scared it may also destroy it. For many weeks she had visited him and helplessly watched as he repeatedly forced his body against the glass wall that stood between them. Each time, she had placed her hands upon the glass, speaking to him in gentle, reassuring tones. He seemed to understand her somehow, and as she moved her hands across the wall he would follow them and become calm.

Jenna loved the aquarium and spent as much time as she could within its comforting walls. She found animals far easier to understand than humans and cherished her work there. The spirited sea otters swam and played in their enclosure. Fidget, however, had struggled to settle in. He had been rescued six months earlier, terrified and weak, stranded on a reef in the nearby bay. Lyla, a sea otter who had lived in the enclosure for many years, was surrogate mother to newly rescued pups and Fidget had begun to bond with her. He also grew stronger each day and his desire for freedom intensified. Despite the barrier between them, Jenna felt a strong connection to Fidget. Perhaps she too craved something she could not reach.

In his quieter moments, Fidget would snuggle closely with Lyla and listen to her stories of the world beyond the enclosure. She described her adventures with other sea otters as they swam and played together in the bay, under the bright, open sky. She spoke proudly of how they had outwitted their predators and survived the powerful wind that lashed across the water, creating colossal, churning waves. As Fidget listened, his eyes full of wonder, he yearned for the life of which she spoke, a life he could not remember. Lyla thrived in her role as mother to the pups that arrived – startled, fearful, in need of love. She felt content in the enclosure, though she knew that Fidget, like others before him, would be released back into the wild when he was ready. She hoped it would bring him the adventure he craved and that he would survive in the ocean without her.

On the day the glass wall cracked and shattered, Fidget was swimming in the clear pool of water, forcing his body against the glass wall, willing it to disappear. A terrifying noise had suddenly echoed around the enclosure as a deep crack worked its way through the glass. Water began to pour out of the pool and there was a deafening shattering of glass. Chaos arose, humans running in all directions, screaming and shouting. Lyla huddled with the other sea otters and watched fearfully as Fidget lay below, on the cold, hard floor of the aquarium. Then she saw him move and relief washed over her. He looked around, eyes wide and alert.

---

* The text of this story can be downloaded and printed at www.pavpub.com/find-your-way-resources

In that moment, he saw the girl who often visited him, the quiet human who would place her hands upon the glass wall that separated them, murmuring comforting words that he did not understand. She was standing by a door, frozen and fearful. He felt he must go to her. Lyla watched anxiously as he moved awkwardly across the wet floor, through the commotion, unnoticed by the other humans. He reached Jenna and she knelt before him, heart pounding, hands trembling. She tentatively stroked his soft coat for the first time and looked into his soulful brown eyes.

The door beside them led to the bay and she felt an urge to open it. Fidget would be free and she would be the one to end his suffering. She stood up slowly and reached for the handle, then hesitated. If she opened the door, she may never see him again, and if somebody saw her she might lose the job that meant so much to her. Then she thought of the powerful ocean and feared what may become of him. How could she know if he was ready? Fidget sensed what lay beyond the door. He looked fondly back at Lyla, then turned again to Jenna. While determined to be free, he felt afraid for the first time. Neither he nor Jenna were sure what to do next…

The story ends here, with both Jenna and Fidget facing a significant choice and Lyla watching on helplessly. Imagine what each of them might be feeling and thinking at this crucial moment?

What would you do if you were in their position?

How do we know when we are ready for the next step of our journey?

How difficult is it to move away from people or places that we feel attached to?

The choice is yours.

Creative activities

Several activities can be offered in relation to *The Glass Wall* and new activities may also be created. The list below describes key exercises that have been used successfully with groups, some of which can be adapted for individual work. You do not have to introduce every activity, nor follow the order in which they are listed. Discussion, however, is often an effective way to begin. The energy or nature of a group – or an individual's initial response to the story – will also guide you towards the most appropriate and effective way of working with it. Some people will feel at ease expressing themselves through artwork, for example, while others will prefer to explore the themes through creative writing. On the other hand, you might have selected this story in order to steer your students or clients in a specific direction – to encourage self-reflection, perhaps. There is no right or wrong way to work with the story, just as there is no right or wrong choice for Fidget and Jenna to make.

Story 6: The Glass Wall

Discussion and choices

After sharing the story with a group, ask them to move into pairs or small groups and encourage them to discuss what they thought about the story and what they think should happen next. If working with an individual, discuss this directly with them. It may help them to consider what they would do if confronted with either Fidget or Jenna's dilemma. You can also ask people to choose a line (or moment) in the story that makes the most impact on them.

It may be helpful to consider the following questions:

1. What would you do if you were in Jenna's position at the point the story pauses? If she opens the door to set Fidget free, she may never see him again and might risk losing the job she loves. She also fears for Fidget's safety. In the aquarium, he was so frustrated that he had begun to force himself repeatedly against the glass wall – yet is he ready to survive in the wild?

2. What would you do if you were in Fidget's position at the point the story pauses? Should he take the opportunity to escape the safety of the aquarium if Jenna opens the door? How might he feel about leaving Lyla, his surrogate mother? He had become frustrated in captivity, but is he truly ready for freedom?

3. How would it feel to be in Lyla's position at the point the story pauses? If Fidget leaves the aquarium, she will never see him again and she fears for his survival in the wild. She also knows how frustrated he has become in the enclosure and wants him to be happy and free.

After these discussions, bring the group back together and invite everyone to share their thoughts. If working in pairs, one approach is to ask each member to say what their partner decided and why. If working with an individual, adapt the process accordingly. It's also important to remember that the choices people make at this point may reflect something significant about their current mood and mental state, or their memories.

Artwork

Invite your students or clients to choose one of the following themes to explore creatively, using whatever art, craft and collage materials are available:

A. Freedom and confinement

B. Attachment and separation

When ready, individuals should be encouraged to present their creations to one another, as this is an important part of the process.

Creative writing

Creative writing in response to *The Glass Wall* works equally well with an individual or a group. There are several helpful strategies which can be used to introduce this activity.

Story 6: The Glass Wall

Ask an individual (or members of a group) to imagine what would happen if the story were to continue. There are several possibilities, some of which may have already been discussed. Participants could either continue to write the narrative or write a monologue for one of the three characters: Fidget, Jenna or Lyla. Monologues allow a character to express their thoughts and feelings in more detail. The points listed in the 'Discussion and Choices' section could be referred to for ideas. If mini scripts or monologues are written, they could then be used for dramatic enactment.

The Glass Wall (tableau sequence)

The six (potentially seven) tableaus described below, can be silent and still, or with simple words, sounds and movement added. Extra tableaus may also be created and lines from the narrative included. Each one can be brought to life in sequence, or a favourite moment chosen and the tableau used as a catalyst for improvisation:

Characters:

- ▶ Fidget – A young sea otter
- ▶ Jenna – A shy young woman who loves animals
- ▶ Lyla – An older sea otter. Surrogate mother to Fidget and others before him.

Other humans and sea otters could be included and director and narrator roles could also be useful.

Tableau 1 – *Fidget and humans from the aquarium:*

Fidget as a pup, stranded on a reef in the bay. He is frightened and alone, his family nowhere in sight. Humans from the aquarium approach him cautiously, planning to rescue him.

Tableau 2 – *Fidget and Jenna (the glass wall separating them):*

Fidget in the sea otter enclosure, his body pressed up against the glass. Jenna puts her hands against the glass, speaking softly to him, calming him down. As she moves her hands across the surface of the glass wall between them, he relaxes and follows.

Tableau 3 – *Fidget and Lyla (other sea otters could be present):*

Fidget snuggles up to Lyla and listens to her stories of life in the ocean.

Tableau 4 – *Fidget, Jenna and Lyla (other humans/sea otters could be present) and sound effects used:*

The glass cracks and shatters. Fidget, whose body had been pressed up against the glass, falls to the aquarium floor, outside of the sea otter enclosure. Lyla and the other otters huddle together, afraid.

Tableau 5 – *Jenna, Fidget and Lyla (other otters/humans too perhaps):*

Jenna kneels before Fidget and strokes his fur for the first time. Lyla is watching on fearfully from the enclosure, huddled with the other sea otters.

Tableau 6 – *Jenna, Fidget and Lyla (other otters/humans too perhaps):*

Jenna reaches for the door handle. Fidget senses what lies beyond the door. He looks affectionately back at Lyla, then returns his gaze to Jenna. He craves freedom yet feels afraid for the first time.

Tableau 7 – *Choose how the story continues and decide what this final tableau should look like!*

Examples of work in practice

The Glass Wall has been used with several client groups. You may discover that, while some people enjoy having a copy of the story to follow, others prefer to relax and listen. Likewise, some might respond well to script work and others will favour a freer, more spontaneous approach. As reflective discussions develop among one group, another will choose to remain in the creative realm. Choice is the prevailing element here, just as in *The Glass Wall*, where Fidget and Jenna have choices to consider and must decide what to do next. It is imperative that everyone is heard and their choices respected. In a group, this could prove challenging at times, and as a facilitator one should try to be as flexible as possible, while encouraging compromise and finding the most appropriate method with which to proceed. Poignant examples follow, in which pseudonyms are used:

Tableaus and improvisation – *Women with schizophrenia*

On the step-down unit for women with mental health difficulties (introduced in chapter 1) *The Glass Wall* was explored over three sessions and was particularly well received. It also inspired two of the participants to create new stories:

1. **Sam** was in her early 30s, diagnosed with paranoid schizophrenia. She was new to the unit and encountered *The Glass Wall* in her first Dramatherapy group. She responded positively to the story and when the group created a tableau to represent the moment when Jenna must decide whether to free Fidget (as Lyla watches on helplessly), she chose to play the role of Jenna – a shy woman who loves animals. At the end of the session, Sam reflected that the story had made her think a lot

about the relationship between humans and animals, which related personally to her own experience of having two pet hamsters. In a further session, Sam was able to express herself through the dramatic process and again connected deeply to *The Glass Wall*. During the dramatic enactment of the moment when Jenna and Fidget communicate through the glass wall, she chose to be Jenna. She found it difficult to improvise dialogue, though afterwards felt confident to create her own story, in which the main character (named Rapunzel) was searching for death in order to reach the afterlife and to escape from the people persecuting her. Her interaction shows how working with one story can inspire people to find their own characters and stories.

2. **Raya** (mentioned in chapters 2 and 3). She was in her early 20s, diagnosed with schizophrenia. During the first session that explored *The Glass Wall*, Raya's mood appeared bright and she focused well, interacting positively with her peers. She chose to take an active role in reading out the narrative and responded reflectively to its themes and characters. In a further session, she again engaged fully and enjoyed the story work. When the group created a tableau to represent the moment that Jenna must decide whether to free Fidget (as Lyla watches on helplessly), Raya chose to play the role of Lyla, surrogate mother to Fidget. At the end of the session, she said she had enjoyed the process and found it interesting. During the final session exploring *The Glass Wall*, Raya was keen to attend, though as the session progressed she appeared to be distracted by her own thoughts. During a dramatic enactment of the moment that Jenna and Fidget communicate through the glass wall, she chose to be Fidget. In role, she improvised some lines and appeared enthusiastic to participate. Suddenly, however, she said that she was not feeling comfortable, apologised to everyone and left the group.

3. **Bailey** (mentioned in chapters 1 and 2) was in her early 30s, diagnosed with schizophrenia and somatic symptoms. She was a deeply spiritual person who felt a powerful connection with nature and birds. In the first session exploring *The Glass Wall*, Bailey engaged well, but appeared to be preoccupied with her diet and the effects of the central heating on her body and digestion. Despite this, she was able to express herself and responded with interest to the story. She missed the group the following week, though came to the third session. Her mood appeared bright and she listened with interest to her peers. During the dramatic enactment of the moment when Jenna and Fidget communicate through the glass wall, Bailey chose to play a wise crow (a new character she created) who witnesses the scene. She later reflected on what the crow's individual story might be. As with Sam, her interaction shows how working with one story can inspire people to find their own characters and new stories.

Artwork and reflection – *Tracey and Anya*

Two service users on the ward for women with EUPD (described in chapter 1) inspired me to write *The Glass Wall*. Both were struggling to prepare for discharge:

1. **Tracey** (mentioned in chapters 1, 3 and 5) attended both sessions that explored *The Glass Wall*. She was one of two individuals who had inspired the story. She found the process of preparing for discharge traumatic, due to a history of neglect and

broken attachments. She responded with great interest to *The Glass Wall* when first hearing it and was able to relate it to her own life. In the next session, she engaged fully and created a piece of artwork to express how it felt to be on 'the current side of the wall' (in hospital) and how it might feel to be on 'the future side of the wall' (in the community). She explained that, while hospital offered care and made her feel safe, the community offered independence and seemed scary. Tracey made great progress and then relapsed before leaving hospital. Eleven months later, she began the process again. It should be noted, however, that many of the clients I have worked with temporarily relapse in the weeks approaching discharge.

2. **Anya** (mentioned in chapters 1 and 5) was the other individual who inspired *The Glass Wall*. She had missed the first session that introduced the story, though came to the second session, in which artwork was encouraged in response to the story's themes. Anya shared that she was finding it challenging to readjust to being on the ward, having spent five days at home. She then engaged fully in the creative process and responded positively to the story of *The Glass Wall*. She used vegetable dough and chosen images to express herself creatively and to reflect on the discharge process and the mix of feelings it stirred. She interacted well with her peers and said at the end that she was very pleased to have come and to have found a way to express how she was feeling. Preparing for discharge unfortunately caused Anya a lot of distress, which then led to a relapse. She was finally discharged to the community, however, 11 months later.

Reference

Morris N (2018) *Dramatherapy for Borderline Personality Disorder: Empowering and Nurturing People through Creativity*. London and New York: Routledge.

Story 7

Silver Angel

Friendship, Transformation and Loss

Illustration by Nicky Morris

Introduction

Silver Angel is the story of a unique friendship that develops between a lonely butterfly and a frustrated caterpillar. Together, they transform one another and their journey addresses the importance of friendship, belonging and the impact of loss. Fundamental to life's journey, mortality, death and grief are themes that cannot be avoided. As Yalom explains, while self-awareness makes us human, it also reminds us of our impermanence: 'Our existence is forever shadowed by the knowledge that we will grow, blossom, and, inevitably, diminish and die' (2008, p1). Our understanding of mortality and potential death anxiety then builds when we are confronted with the death of a loved one.

Many of the young women I work with struggle to cope with issues around death. Several mourn for friends or family members who have committed suicide or died from natural causes, while others battle with suicidal thoughts and remain ambivalent about life (Morris, 2018, chapter 7). Gersie describes the complex emotions, even terror, that can be experienced when losing a loved one. She also notes the impossibility of preparing for its impact. She suggests that 'Death is the great expected unexpected. It is the anticipated yet unknown journey' (1991, p30). Using stories to support people through bereavement, Gersie explains how stories were formed and have been shared since ancient times to help us to understand and accept the reality of death (1991, p55).

The silver butterfly in the story has traumatic dreams that she does not understand. She also feels isolated and inferior to those around her. Her mental state has echoes of PTSD (post-traumatic stress disorder) which stem from her experience of metamorphosis. The caterpillar, however, sees only how beautiful she is and senses immediately that she can help him somehow. A genuine friendship then develops. The silver butterfly is finally able to embrace her new self and to make sense of her past. She is then able to support the caterpillar when his chrysalis begins to form. Aspects of their journey then mirror the loss that may be experienced as we move from one stage of life to the next, and the challenges that new stages can bring.

I have explored the theme of loss with many clients (in both group and individual Dramatherapy sessions). Story and metaphor offer an alternative form through which to find personal meaning. Several clients are referred for 1:1 bereavement-focused sessions, for example, and Silver Angel has become a very useful tool. Before working with the story, you might want to read more about the butterfly's lifecycle and metamorphosis (Ballard, 2014).

Metamorphosis

This activity works well as a warm-up exercise before introducing the *Silver Angel* story, but could also be used at a later stage of the process:

Invite your clients or students to find a space where they have enough room to stretch out their arms and legs. Explain that you are going to talk them through a dramatic exercise, during which they will imagine themselves moving through the four stages of a butterfly's lifecycle. They should be encouraged to use their bodies to express themselves, in response to the instructions. Please note, however, that the activity can also be adapted to suit individual needs or physical restrictions, for example. Different music can be played to accompany the four stages of the lifecycle and, from the beginning, each person could choose a large coloured feather, a piece of material or a shawl, for example, to hold or wear around them. Props and music do not have to be used, though can enhance the sensory element of the activity:

Stage 1 – Imagine that you are a tiny egg, unborn, unaware of life. How does this feel?

Stage 2 – You are now ready to hatch and emerge from your egg as a caterpillar. Picture what colour you are. How do you feel? You are probably very hungry and you need to eat in order to grow.

Stage 3 – You are now a fully grown caterpillar and it's time to rest. You attach yourself to a leaf and shed your final layer. Under your skin, a chrysalis has formed. Inside the cocoon, a great transformation begins. It might be uncomfortable, even painful. How do you feel?

Stage 4 – Metamorphosis is complete and you break free from your chrysalis, emerging as newly born butterfly. Your wings are initially soft. They begin to beat, then grow stronger, as your body prepares itself to take flight for the first time. How do you feel?

Following the activity, invite the participants to discuss how they found the experience (as a group, in pairs or in smaller groups). How did they feel in each of the four stages? Was there one stage they preferred or one they found more difficult than the others, for example?

Before facilitating this activity, you might want to read about the butterfly's lifecycle and metamorphosis (*Joyful Butterfly*, 2014).

Silver Angel (narrative)[7]

She fluttered in the breeze, looking down at the earth below, yearning to land. She was exhausted. There was so much to fear – the powerful wind, the freezing rain and the ravenous birds and spiders. She was also disturbed by vivid memories, in which she was wingless, wriggling through the dirt. She bore little resemblance to the creature of her dreams and yet the dusty earth felt so familiar, as did the incessant hunger.

She encountered other butterflies on her journey, each so beautiful and unique. They appeared effortless to her and she wondered if they too had these visions. She also wished she could embrace life as they did and could worry less about the dangers of the world. She envied their beauty and their ease. Their wings shone with vibrant colours and intricate markings. She was so different to them – her plain, pale grey wings, her debilitating fear. To make things worse, they seemed to laugh whenever they saw her, which she thought must be due to her lack of colour and courage. She therefore isolated herself, flying alone, watching others from a distance.

As her wings grew tired, she settled in a meadow brimming with sunflowers, rich with nectar. At last, she could rest. She drank thirstily, then focused on the sounds

---

* The text of this story can be downloaded and printed at www.pavpub.com/find-your-way-resources

around her, whilst allowing her wings to absorb the sun's rays. She was glad to have a moment of peace.

Nearby, a young caterpillar with amber stripes searched for milk clover. His appetite was relentless and he longed for a companion. As he crawled in the dirt, he wished his hunger would cease. He paused for a moment, looking up at the expansive sky, and in that moment he saw her! She fluttered down from the heavens and settled daintily on the brightest sunflower. As she bathed in the sunlight, the silver tones of her delicate wings glistened like gems. She was exquisite, a vision of beauty and freedom. He was mesmerised, his hunger and frustration finally abating. He sensed that she had the answers he was looking for and crawled tentatively towards her.

'What are you?' asked the caterpillar.

'I don't really know', answered the butterfly.

'I saw you fly down from the heavens, like a silver angel.' She smiled and, peering more closely at him, said, 'You remind me of the creature in my dreams.'

He blushed.

'Do you know what you are?' she asked.

The caterpillar thought for a moment, then answered, 'I'm always hungry and I crawl the earth in search of food. That's who I am.'

An understanding settled between them and they fell into a comfortable silence, breathing in the same crisp, fresh air. They felt safe together somehow, as though a missing piece had been found.

Over the next few days, the caterpillar and the butterfly grew close. They laughed and played, the butterfly no longer so afraid and the caterpillar less agitated. They remained together for many weeks, guiding and supporting one another. They moved around the meadow together, looking for milk clover and shading from the wind and rain under the golden canopy of sunflowers. Other creatures in the meadow smiled when they saw them together, with such joy and ease between them. The butterfly began to have a new dream, in which she was encased in a cocoon, her body changing. She broke free and tried to follow others that looked like her, but couldn't keep up and found herself alone.

One morning, she woke from her dream to the desperate cries of her new young friend.

'Help … help!'

He was hanging from a shining leaf beneath the bloom on which she rested.

'What's happening to me?'

He was moulting, his final layer shedding, the chrysalis under his skin taking shape.

'I'm afraid', he whimpered.

As the butterfly stared at her friend, memories of her time in the cocoon came flooding back.

'It's time to change, my friend. Everything will be okay.'

'I don't understand', he said.

'I remember now, caterpillar. I was once like you and then I transformed. I grew these wings and took to the sky.'

'I don't want to change', he said. 'I want to stay here with you.'

'I'll watch over you, caterpillar. Don't be afraid. I'll stay here until you're reborn', she added. 'I was frightened of everything before we met and you taught me to be brave. Now it's your turn.'

The caterpillar began to relax, allowing the chrysalis to take shape around him. He felt a little afraid, though also excited, as he knew that soon he would be with his silver butterfly and together they would fly.

Ten days later, he broke free from the walls of his cocoon and slowly stretched out his soft, new, amber wings. He looked around eagerly for his friend. She lay motionless on a leaf nearby. He moved tentatively towards her. She remained frozen, her pale wings no longer fluttering. Her body was cold and he began to cry, the tears flowing with a force so strong he thought they may never stop. He lay beside her, his wings beginning to throb, his body preparing for flight. Yet he did not move; he did not want to fly.

He had allowed his body and mind to transform. He had found the energy to break free from his chrysalis. He had survived his transformation and now he was alone again. It seemed that his struggle on the earth and in the cocoon had been in vain and a fog of hopelessness engulfed him. He could smell the scent of others like him nearby, though he did not want to find them and did not want to be found. He lay beside his silver angel and hoped that he too would grow cold, his new wings never to flutter. His sadness then turned to anger. He did not know why she had died and blamed himself for leaving her alone. He would never leave her again.

He closed his eyes and dreamt about his silver angel. When he woke however, he noticed something he had not seen before: a gathering of tiny eggs, just beneath her pale grey wing. His spirits lifted a little and he considered the choices before him. Should he continue to lie beside his friend, depriving himself of nectar and waiting for the sleep of death to take him? Or should he take care of her eggs and protect her offspring? Maybe he could seek help or advice from another creature and perhaps one day he would feel able to make a new life for himself? Unsure if he had the strength of mind and body for such an adventure, he imagined what his silver angel would say to him in this moment.

Story 7: Silver Angel

The story pauses here.

The newly born amber butterfly faces the loss of his friend and the prospect of life without her.

How will he cope and what will he do?

The choice is yours.

Creative activities

Several activities can be offered in relation to *Silver Angel* and new activities may also be created. Key exercises will be described that have been used successfully with groups. Some can also be adapted for individual work. You do not have to introduce every activity, nor follow the order in which they are listed. Discussion, however, is often an effective way to begin. The energy or nature of a group – or an individual's initial response to the story – will also guide you towards the most appropriate and effective way of working with it. Some people enjoy participating in dramatic enactment work, for example, while others may feel more at ease with expressing themselves through artwork. On the other hand, you might have selected this story in order to steer your students or clients in a specific direction – to encourage creative writing, for example. There is no right or wrong way to work with the story, just as there is no right or wrong choice for the newly born amber butterfly to make.

Discussion and questions

After sharing *Silver Angel*, discuss the arising themes and possible choices for the amber butterfly. If there are more than six participants, splitting into pairs or smaller groups may be useful. Encourage people to discuss what they thought about the story and to consider what they would like to happen next. It may help them to reflect on what they would do if facing the situation. When working with an individual, adapt the process accordingly. Where the narrative ends, Amber Butterfly is left contemplating what to do with his life now that his friend (Silver Angel) has died. He considers several options for participants to explore:

1. Will he continue to lie beside his friend, neglecting himself and waiting for the sleep of death?
2. Will he look after himself, so that he can protect his Silver Angel's eggs?
3. Will he seek help or advice from another creature?
4. Will he feel able to create a new life for himself one day, with new friends in a new place?
5. What do you think Silver Angel would have wanted Amber Butterfly to do after her death?

Following these discussions, bring the group back together and invite everyone to share their thoughts. If working in pairs, one approach is to ask each member to say what their partner decided and why. It is again important to remember that the choices people make at this point are likely to reflect something significant about their current mood and mental state, or even their memories.

As well as considering Amber Butterfly's choices at the end of the story, there are key themes to explore and discuss:

1. Feeling different, fearful, frustrated or isolated.
2. The significance of friendship and how others may see us differently to how we see ourselves.
3. The challenge of transformation – transitioning from one phase of life to the next.
4. The impact of losing a loved one and coping with grief.

Invite your students or clients to consider which of these themes they most relate to. They can also choose a key moment or a line from the narrative which makes the most impact on them.

Artwork

Invite your clients or students to use whatever arts, crafts and collage materials are available to create their own butterfly and caterpillar (2D or 3D). Explain that the caterpillar can represent their current self and the butterfly may symbolise their hopes and dreams. The idea is that transformation is possible for everyone and even for those who are happy as they are, change will come, as people grow older and new challenges arise. Colours and patterns can be used to symbolise emotion and personality, for example. Once finished, encourage participants to show one another their artwork, as sharing and witnessing each other's creations is an important part of the process. This activity is equally effective for both individual and group work.

Creative writing

A helpful strategy to introduce creative writing is to ask an individual (or members of a group) to imagine what would happen if the *Silver Angel* story were to continue. There are several possibilities and it may be helpful to refer to both the options and the key themes (listed in the 'Discussion and Choices' section). This activity works equally well with an individual or group and you can offer your participants the following options:

1. Continue to write the narrative version of the story.
2. Create a mini script.
3. Write a monologue for the newly born Amber Butterfly.

Silver Angel (tableau sequence)

This sequence highlights key moments of the story. Dramatic tableaus can be silent and still, or simple words, sounds and movement may be added. Narrator lines and dialogue can also be improvised, devised or taken from the narrative (as shown below). Other key moments may be identified, with additional tableaus created. Props, costume and sound effects may be used to enhance the process.

Tableau 1	**Narrator and Silver Angel** (plus other Butterflies)
Narrator:	She fluttered in the breeze, exhausted, alone and fearful. Other butterflies flew past, each one beautiful and unique.
Silver Angel:	My wings are grey and I'm afraid of everything. I wish I could be more like them.
Tableau 2	**Narrator, Caterpillar and Silver Angel**
Narrator:	A frustrated, hungry caterpillar looked up at the sky and was amazed to see a silver angel flutter down from the heavens and settle on the brightest sunflower.
Caterpillar:	She's exquisite, so beautiful and free.
Tableau 3	**Silver Angel, Caterpillar and Narrator**
Caterpillar:	What are you?
Silver Angel:	I don't really know.
Caterpillar:	I saw you fly down from the heavens, like a silver angel.
Silver Angel:	*(Smiles)* You remind me of the creature in my dreams. Do you know what you are?
Caterpillar:	*(Pauses)* I'm always hungry and I crawl the earth in search of food. That's who I am.
Narrator:	An understanding settled between them and they fell into a comfortable silence. They felt safe together somehow, as though a missing piece had been found.
Tableau 4	**Narrator (Silver Angel and Caterpillar)**
Narrator:	The caterpillar and butterfly grew close. They laughed and played together in the meadow, the butterfly no longer so afraid and the caterpillar less agitated. They stayed together for many weeks, guiding and supporting one another.

Tableau 5	Narrator, Silver Angel and Caterpillar
Narrator:	One morning, the butterfly woke to the desperate cries of the caterpillar.
Caterpillar:	Help … help! What's happening to me? I'm afraid.
Silver Angel:	It's time to change, my friend. Everything will be okay.
Caterpillar:	I don't understand.
Silver Angel:	I remember now, caterpillar. I was once like you and then I transformed. I grew these wings and took to the sky.
Caterpillar:	I don't want to change. I want to stay here with you.
Silver Angel:	I'll watch over you, caterpillar. Don't be afraid. I'll stay here until you're reborn. I was frightened of everything before we met and you taught me to be brave. Now it's your turn.
Narrator:	So, he began to relax, allowing the chrysalis to take shape around him. He felt a little afraid, though also excited, knowing that he would soon be able to fly with his silver angel.
Tableau 6	Narrator (Silver Angel and Caterpillar)
Narrator:	Ten days later, he broke free from his cocoon and stretched out his soft, new amber wings. He looked around for his friend and saw her lying on a leaf nearby. He approached her and found her body cold, her wings no longer fluttering. He began to cry, the tears flowing with a force so strong he thought they may never stop. He lay beside her, his wings throbbing, preparing for flight, yet he did not want to move.
Tableau 7	Narrator (Silver Angel and Caterpillar)
Narrator:	The caterpillar had survived his transformation and now he was alone again. He lay beside his silver angel and hoped that he too would grow cold. He blamed himself for leaving her alone and vowed he would never leave her again. He then noticed a gathering of tiny eggs just beneath one of her silver wings. His spirits lifted and unsure what to do next, he imagined what his silver angel would say to him in this moment.

Examples of work in practice

Silver Angel has been particularly useful in bereavement-focused work with individuals. It has also been explored successfully with groups. You may discover that while some people enjoy having a copy of the story to follow, others prefer to relax and listen. Likewise, some might respond well to script work and others will favour a freer, more spontaneous approach. As reflective discussions develop among one group, another will choose to remain in the creative realm. Choice is the prevailing element here, just as in *Silver Angel*, where the newly born Amber Butterfly has several choices to consider and must decide what to do next. It is imperative that everyone is heard and their choices respected. In a group this could prove challenging at times and as a facilitator one should try to be as flexible as possible, while encouraging compromise and finding the most appropriate method with which to proceed.

A poignant example follows, in which a pseudonym is used:

Grief – A young woman with PTSD

I met Roxanne on the specialist ward for women diagnosed with EUPD (described in chapter 1). She was in her early 20s, diagnosed with EUPD (emotionally unstable personality disorder) and PTSD (post-traumatic stress disorder). Her symptoms included severe depressive episodes, intense flashbacks and both visual and auditory hallucinations. She responded with serious self-harm (such as headbanging) and suicide attempts (including ligatures and overdoses). Aside from her difficulties, she was a gifted artist, singer and poet, who quickly became a committed member of the weekly Dramatherapy group, expressive art and writing group and therapeutic music group.

After her first couple of weeks on the ward, it became evident that Roxanne would benefit from 1:1 bereavement-focused work, within a creative (Dramatherapy) structure. She was keen to engage in this work and attended weekly 1:1 sessions for four months. Roxanne responded positively to story work, in both group and individual sessions. *Little Blue* was the first of the stories she encountered (in the creative art and writing group). During her third 1:1 bereavement-focused session, her mood was clearly low and she shared that her suicidal urges were high. The first anniversary of a close friend's suicide was approaching and she acknowledged her spiritual concerns around this, adding that she continued to struggle to accept her friend's death. *The Lost One* was then introduced, as a creative tool through which Roxanne could reflect further on her current state of mind. She found this very useful.

Roxanne once explained that as a young child, she had learnt to internalise unpleasant feelings, until they grew so intense that they exploded. She described the sensation of suppressing her feelings as 'screaming on the inside'. A few years earlier, she had experienced another loss, which triggered ongoing grief, confusion, shame, regret and fear. She had also endured an abusive childhood, fraught with parental conflict. I originally wrote *Silver Angel* to help Roxanne to come to terms with her friend's death. We read the story together in her final 1:1 bereavement-focused session. She responded thoughtfully, then tearfully expressed her desire to die. Emotions were perhaps intensified, however, as it was our last session and trust had developed. Loss had become a running theme in Roxanne's life and consequently attachment and separation remained challenging.

In this final 1:1 session, *Silver Angel* allowed Roxanne to explore alternatives to focusing on death as a solution to intense grief and to consider what her friend would want her to do. After the session, she was encouraged to continue attending the creative therapy groups and to use her creative skills to express herself between sessions (as well as speaking to staff) rather than allow her negative feelings and thoughts to build up inside, without release.

Roxanne drew the following illustration in response to the story *Silver Angel*.

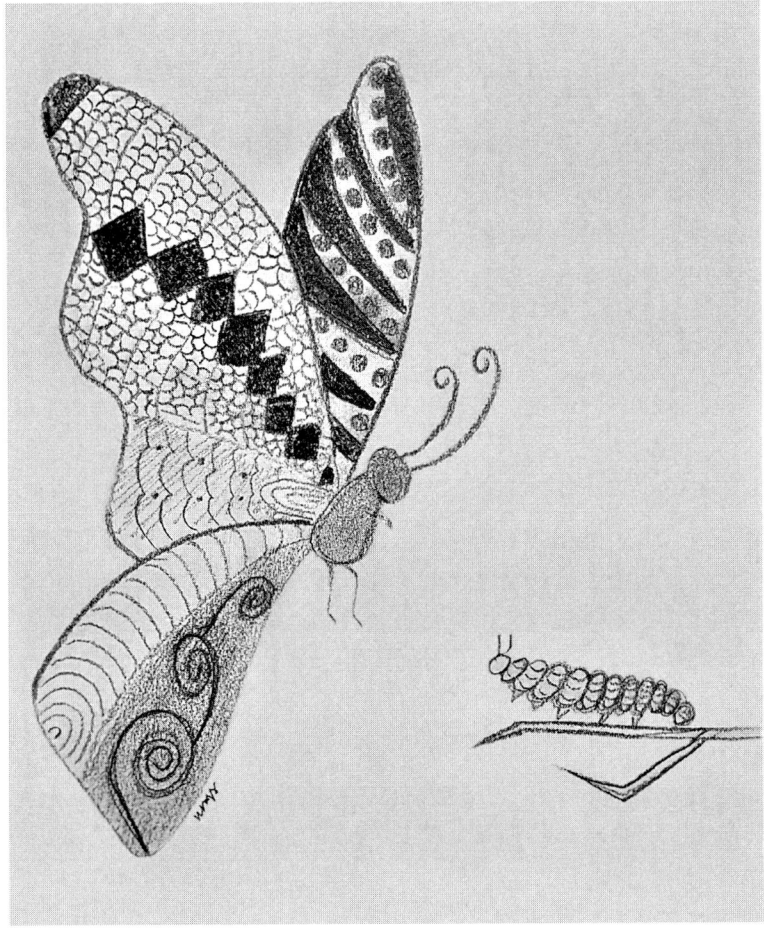

References

Ballard K (2014) Life Cycle of a Butterfly: Amazing! *Joyful Butterfly*. Available at: https://www.joyfulbutterfly.com/life-cycle-of-a-butterfly/

Gersie A (1991) *Storymaking in Bereavement: Dragons Fight in the Meadow*. London and Philadelphia: Jessica Kingsley Publishers.

Holloway P (2011) Surviving suicide: The book of life and death. In: D Dokter, P Holloway and H Seebohm (Eds) *Dramatherapy and Destructiveness: Creating the Evidence Base, Playing with Thanatos* (Kindle edition). London: Taylor & Francis.

Roxanne (pseudonym) (2019) Written permission to use her illustration and case vignette. Yalom I (2008) *Staring at the Sun: Overcoming the Dread of Death* (Kindle edition). London: Hachette Digital.

Story 8

Born of Shadow and Light

Emotional Balance

Illustration by Rhiannon Mcintosh Azzoun

Introduction

Born of Shadow and Light is essentially about working towards inner balance and may be considered in relation to Jungian psychology. Jung hypothesised that in addition to the Core Self, there exists in each of us the following archetypal parts: Ego, Persona, Shadow and Anima or Animus. His belief was that they contribute to psychic development and social adjustment, and whilst part of all people, they are experienced uniquely (Stevens, 2001, p61). Understanding them may then help us to live a more genuine, fulfilling life.

The Shadow part is most relevant to the story *Born of Shadow and Light*. It relates to the idea that in order to feel emotionally balanced and authentic, we must try to acknowledge and accept our internal Shadow part. This often becomes more challenging after we enter puberty and later emerge as adults. McNiff suggests that intense negative emotions, often contributing to our shadow part, may be an essential source of creativity. He also explains that such feelings need recognition and release, enabling them to eventually compliment the lighter aspects of self (2015, p119). Jung theorised that when we suppress and deny our internal Shadow, we unconsciously project it onto others, which can lead to significant problems on an individual or even societal level (Stevens, 2001, pp64–67).

Born of Shadow and Light features two central characters, who may symbolise two halves of the same person, or perhaps two individuals: one who has suppressed their Shadow part in an effort to experience life with less pain; the other who is overly connected to their Shadow part and therefore unable to experience the lighter, brighter aspects of life. Their characters may also be considered in relation to Yin and Yang, the ancient philosophy central to Chinese culture. In simple terms, Yin and Yang exist in every aspect of life, as both inseparable and contradictory elements. They are of equal importance and, as Cartwright explains, 'a correct balance between the two poles must be reached in order to achieve harmony' (2018). Many of the young women I work with have experienced extreme trauma, and those with EUPD (emotionally unstable personality disorder) in particular express an ambivalence towards life, fluctuating between the desire to live and a yearning for death. The emotional pain they experience, whether in response to their past or present, may also have a considerable impact on those working with them (Morris, 2018, chapter 7). It is perhaps overidentification with their shadow part that overwhelms the lighter parts within their psyche.

The story of Lumo (the child of light) and Ombro (the child of shadow) may also lead to an exploration of 'relationship'. It is important to note, however, that while Lumo is referred to as 'he' and Ombro as 'she', this is not fixed and both characters may be of either gender and any sexual orientation. The importance of forming and maintaining genuine relationships (platonic and/or romantic) is a secondary theme in the story, as our ability to connect with others may also help us to feel more balanced and content. Jung also recognised the importance of relationship and how men and women relate to one another. He suggested that every man has an inner anima (a feminine part) and every woman has an inner animus (a masculine part). He also considered the archetypal significance of both the masculine and the feminine, seeing them as equal, complementary parts, helping to balance the universe (Stevens, 2001, pp70–1).

The names Lumo and Ombro were chosen from the Esperanto language, translating respectively as light and shadow. In relation to the key themes of communication and balance, choosing Esperanto words has further significance. Zamenhof – who developed the language in the late 1800s – grew up in a town in the Russian Empire (now part of Poland), witnessing fear and mistrust between its different ethnic communities, each with separate cultures and languages. He was a sensitive idealist who wanted to offer the world a simple, constructive second language, free from political undertones, which would help to improve communication and ease future tensions in Europe and across the world (Richardson, 2017, pp15–17).

Before sharing the story with a group, you could invite your students or clients to imagine that they have entered the Maze of Beginnings, in which opposites can be explored. If you are working in a studio space, people can actively participate and you can place chairs or beanbags around the space, for example. Invite them to walk through the maze, as individuals or in pairs, suggesting contrasting styles in which to move; arouse their imaginations by adding environmental factors such as temperature, weather and changes to the ground beneath them. Differing emotions can also be added. Following this opening activity, share the story.

While sharing the story (for the first or second time), encourage your students or clients to respond spontaneously to key moments, using sound (voice and/or percussion), props (such as material and ribbon wands) and simple movement. This activity gently encourages self-expression.

Born of Shadow and Light (narrative)[8]

The Spirit of the Earth smiled as she watched Lumo, the child of light, and Ombro, the child of shadow, walk hand in hand through the Maze of Beginnings.

When the sun shone, Lumo laughed and taught his shadow friend how to skip. When it rained, Ombro showed her light companion how to weep. In the midst of a storm, they huddled closely, protecting one another, then watched in wonder as a rainbow emerged. Beautiful colours born out of the darkness, fear and hope uniting. Whatever they faced, they did so together, and balance remained.

As time passed, however, the maze grew more intricate and new challenges arose. They found it increasingly difficult to stay on the same path and as Lumo began to float just above the earth, Ombro sank a little into its depths. Eventually, the space between them grew into a void and they lost sight of one another.

The Spirit of the Earth watched and wept.

In her new solitude, Ombro began to write poetry so deep and dark that others cried when they read them. Her poems helped them to connect to their most troubling feelings and memories, offering them much needed support. As she roamed the Earth, she witnessed the relentless brutality of humankind and her soul began to overflow with fury, like a volcano. Anger and frustration fuelled her towards rebellion and while

---

* The text of this story can be downloaded and printed at www.pavpub.com/find-your-way-resources

her passionate speeches inspired positive change, each time she won a battle, she craved another fight. She became so volatile that even those who respected her kept their distance. She therefore continued her journey alone.

On the other side of the world, Lumo wrote songs filled with hope and light. He sang for happy crowds and spent time with those who embraced the lighter side of life. As he danced across the Earth, he saw the beauty of the world and avoided suffering by denying the pain that others felt. He too remained alone on his journey, however, in a conscious effort to avoid personal loss, rejection or confrontation. He did not allow himself to become too close to anyone and continuously travelled to new places in search of fresh adventure and inspiration. He wanted to show others the beauty and light in the world, but felt impotent in the face of sadness and pain.

The child of light and the child of shadow now stood on opposite sides of the Earth. They no longer remembered one another and yet each knew that something was missing. As the years passed, Ombro sank deeper into despair, while Lumo floated yet further away from anything that might disturb his happiness. After they heard the news that a full solar eclipse was coming, they both travelled to the mountain from which it would be most visible, and it was here that their paths finally crossed.

Ombro stood at the edge of the mountain, staring beyond the ocean, her arms stretched out, the wind slapping her face. Lumo climbed the same winding path and, upon reaching the top, was shocked to see a young person standing so precariously close to the edge. He felt a surge of confusing emotions, wanting to slip away silently, yet also fascinated and unable to move. The moon began to glide across the disc of the sun and Ombro trembled as the sky darkened, the temperature fell and silence filled the air. She moved even closer to the cliff's edge and breathed in deeply. The moon now covered the disc of the sun completely and only its corona remained visible.

In this beautiful yet eerie moment, Lumo felt compelled to speak.

'Why are you standing so close to the edge?' he gently said.

Ombro turned in surprise, astonished to see another person standing just a few metres from her.

'I want to be as close as possible to this beautiful moment.'

Lumo again felt conflicted. He wanted to run away yet remained rooted to the ground. He sensed that she needed him there and that somehow, he needed her too. Ombro was also shaken by their encounter. She had come to the mountain's edge to enjoy her solitude and to bask in the darkness of the eclipse, yet she now stood facing a young person whose eyes shone with light, despite the darkness that engulfed them. As they continued to stare at one another, the sun began to re-emerge from behind the moon and a wave of familiarity washed over them.

The Spirit of the Earth watched and smiled.

Lumo walked slowly over to Ombro and offered her his hand. He felt anxious, unsure if it was the right thing to do and sensing that this moment could change him forever. Ombro tentatively moved her hand towards to his, then hesitated, as she too felt the significance of the moment and feared she was not ready to step away from the edge.

Lumo and Ombro's story pauses here and it is for you to decide what happens next.

They face a significant choice, as taking hold of one another's hands in this moment may take them on a new path, away from what has become familiar.

There is no right or wrong choice to make. They may or may not be ready.

Whatever they decide, the paths of light and shadow will continue to cross, just as there will be further eclipses.

Creative activities

In response to *Born of Shadow and Light*, many paths can be explored through discussion, then ideas and characters developed through improvisation, creative writing, roleplay and script work. New activities may also be created. The list below describes key exercises that have been used successfully with groups, and some can be adapted for individual work. You do not have to introduce every activity, nor follow the order in which they are listed. Discussion, however, is often an effective way to begin. The energy or nature of a group – or an individual's initial response to the story – will also guide you towards the most appropriate and effective way of working with it. Some people enjoy expressing themselves through creative writing, for example, while others may prefer dramatic enactment. On the other hand, you might have selected this story in order to steer your students or clients in a specific direction – to encourage self-reflection for example. There is no right or wrong way to work with the story, just as there are no right or wrong choices for Lumo and Ombro:

Discussion and choices

After sharing *Born of Shadow and Light* with a group, ask them to move into pairs or small groups and encourage them to discuss what they thought about the story and to consider what they would like to happen next. If working with an individual, adapt the process accordingly. It may help them to reflect on what they would do if they were in either Lumo or Ombro's position.

The following questions will be helpful:

- ▶ Will Lumo and Ombro join hands at the cliff's edge?
- ▶ Whether they reunite or remain apart, what would you like to happen next?
- ▶ If they join hands, do you think they will remember their childhood together?

- Why do you think Lumo and Ombro found life challenging without one another?
- If Lumo and Ombro reconnect, how might they be able to help one another?
- Choose the moment in the story that has the most meaning for you.
- From a personal perspective, what would you like to take away from the story?

After these discussions, bring the group back together and invite everyone to share their thoughts. You can also ask each person to identify the moment or line from the story that makes the most impact on them. If working in pairs, one approach is to ask each member to say what their partner decided and why. It is also important to remember that the choices people make at this point may reflect something significant about their current mood and mental state, or their memories.

Artwork

Invite your clients or students to create a piece of artwork, using whatever art and craft materials are available. It could symbolise:

A. The character to which they feel most connected.

B. A significant theme.

C. A chosen moment from the story.

If working with a group, encourage your clients or students to show one another their artwork when ready, as sharing and witnessing each other's creations is an important part of the process. This activity is appropriate for both group and individual work.

Dramatic tableaus

In pairs, work through the key moments of the story by creating simple tableaus together. One person can take on the role of Ombro and the other the role of Lumo. If you have an odd number, you can include the Spirit of the Earth character. Words and movement may also be added.

Creative writing

A helpful strategy to introduce creative writing is to ask an individual (or members of a group) to imagine what would happen if the story were to continue. There are several possibilities and the questions listed in the 'Discussion and Choices' section may be helpful. Participants could continue to write the narrative version of the story or the mini script that follows. Alternatively, they might prefer to write a monologue for one (or more) of the characters. Creative writing works equally well with an individual or group.

Born of Shadow and Light (mini script)

There are five mini-scenes and three characters (male or female) that could be played by different people in each scene. Spirit Earth acts as a Narrator. Large groups could also split into smaller groups, however, taking one scene each, for example. There are three characters in scenes 1, 2 and 5, and only two characters in scenes 3 and 4. Director, design and sound effects roles could also be added. Stage directions are suggested in italics.

Scene 1	3 Characters: Spirit Earth, Lumo and Ombro
Spirit Earth:	Lumo, the child of light, and Ombro, the child of shadow, walked hand in hand, through the Maze of Beginnings.
Lumo:	*(Smiling and excited)* Ombro, the sun is shining.
Ombro:	*(Nervous)* What should we do?
Lumo:	*(Happily)* Let's skip together! *(They laugh and skip together)*
Ombro:	*(Smiling and relaxed)* It's raining now, Lumo.
Lumo:	*(Nervous)* What should we do?
Ombro:	*(Calmly)* Let's cry together. *(They cry together and storm sound effects gradually build)*
Lumo:	I'm frightened, Ombro, what is it?
Ombro:	I think it's a storm, stay close to me.
Spirit Earth:	As the storm crashed around them, they huddled closely, protecting one another. *(Storm sounds fade out and a rainbow appears)*
Lumo:	It's so beautiful.
Ombro:	What is it, Lumo?
Lumo:	I think it's a rainbow – the light of the sun is shining through the raindrops.
Ombro:	It looks as though our tears and laughter have come together in the sky. *(They watch the rainbow in wonder)*
Spirit Earth:	Whatever they faced, they did so together, and balance remained.
Scene 2	3 Characters: Spirit Earth, Lumo and Ombro
Spirit Earth:	As time passed, the maze grew more intricate and new challenges arose.
Lumo:	*(Happy and excited)* Look at me, Ombro, I'm floating!

Story 8: Born of Shadow and Light

Ombro:	Wait, Lumo! I'm sinking a little and it's difficult to keep up with you.
Lumo:	*(Excited)* Hurry, Ombro! I can't stop floating, come with me.
Ombro:	*(Frustrated)* I'm trying, Lumo! I can't help sinking, stay with me.
Spirit Earth:	*(Sadly)* They found it increasingly difficult to remain on the same path and eventually, the space between them grew into a void and they lost sight of one another.
Scene 3	2 Characters: Spirit Earth and Ombro
Spirit Earth:	Ombro was alone. She began to write poetry so deep and dark that people cried when they read it. She then roamed the Earth and was shocked to witness the brutality of humankind.
Ombro:	*(Passionate)* My soul overflows with fury.
Spirit Earth:	Anger and frustration fuelled her towards rebellion.
Ombro:	My passionate speeches inspire positive change, yet each time I win a battle, I crave another fight.
Spirit Earth:	She became so volatile that even those who respected her kept their distance and she continued her journey alone.
Scene 4	2 Characters: Spirit Earth and Lumo
Spirit Earth:	On the other side of the world, Lumo wrote songs filled with hope and light. He sang for happy crowds and spent time with those who embraced the lighter side of life.
Lumo:	I dance across the Earth and see the beauty of the world.
Spirit Earth:	He avoided suffering by denying the pain that others felt and never allowed himself to become too close to anyone.
Lumo:	I travel to new places in search of fresh adventure and inspiration.
Spirit Earth:	He felt impotent in the face of sadness and pain.
Lumo:	I want to show people the light and beauty in the world.
Spirit Earth:	So, he too remained alone on his journey, consciously avoiding loss, rejection and confrontation.
Scene 5	3 Characters: Spirit Earth, Lumo and Ombro
Spirit Earth:	The child of light and the child of shadow stood on opposites

sides of the Earth. They no longer remembered one another and yet each felt that something was missing. After they heard that a full solar eclipse was coming, both travelled to the mountain from which it would be most visible, and it was here that their paths finally crossed.

Ombro: *(Stands at the mountain's edge, staring beyond the ocean, her arms stretched out)* I'm here.

Lumo: *(Arrives just after Ombro and stands several metres behind her)* I've arrived.

Spirit Earth: The moon began to glide across the disc of the sun.

Ombro: It's amazing! *(She moves even closer to the edge and breathes in deeply)*

Spirit Earth: Ombro trembled as the sky darkened, the temperature fell and silence filled the air. The moon now covered the disk of the sun completely.

Lumo: Why are you standing so close to the edge?

Ombro: *(Turns in surprise, having thought she was alone)* I want to be as close as possible to this beautiful moment.

Spirit Earth: Lumo wanted to run away, yet remained rooted to the ground. He sensed that she needed him there, and that somehow, he needed her too.

Ombro: I came here to be alone and to enjoy the darkness of the eclipse. Why are you here?

Lumo: I came to see if the sun could truly be concealed.

Spirit Earth: Ombro was shaken by their encounter, though fascinated by Lumo's eyes, which shone with light despite the darkness. As they stared at one another, the sun began to re-emerge from behind the moon and a wave of familiarity washed over them. Lumo walked slowly over to Ombro and offered her his hand. She tentatively moved her hand towards his, then hesitated, unsure if she was ready to step away from the edge.

Examples of work in practice

Born of Shadow and Light has been used with several client groups and many individuals. You may discover that, while some people enjoy having a copy of the story to follow, others prefer to relax and listen. Likewise, some might respond well to script work and others will favour a freer, more spontaneous approach. As reflective discussions develop among one group, another will choose to remain in the creative realm. Choice is the prevailing element here, just as in *Born of Shadow and Light*, where Lumo and Ombro face a significant choice at the end of their story and are free to decide what to do next. It is imperative that everyone is heard and their choices respected. In a group, this could prove challenging at times, and as a facilitator one should try to be as flexible as possible, while encouraging compromise and finding the most appropriate method with which to proceed. Poignant examples follow, in which pseudonyms are used:

Wendy and Anna – *Eating disorders ward*

I worked with Anna (mentioned in chapters 2 and 5) and Wendy on a specialist female eating disorders ward. Both were just 20 years old. Wendy was diagnosed with anorexia nervosa and EUPD (emotionally unstable personality disorder) and Anna with PAWS (pervasive arousal withdrawal syndrome). They attended several Dramatherapy groups together and responded well to the creative process. *Born of Shadow and Light* was the first of the stories introduced to Wendy and both clients found it thought provoking and emotive. When first sharing the story, we sat on the floor in a circle and a spontaneous activity developed: We used our fingers to symbolise the characters in the story, moving them in response to each step of the journey. The following week, we explored the mini script and brought it to life using a few simple props and material. Anna chose to be Lumo, Wendy chose Spirit Earth and I read the part of Ombro. Again, this was accomplished while sitting on the floor in a circle. Both activities reveal the potential for dramatic enactment to take a more subtle form, allowing people of all needs and abilities to participate.

Full dramatic enactment – Female mental health rehab

Born of Shadow and Light was explored over several sessions with a group of women on a secure step-down unit (described in chapter 1). Most of the women were diagnosed with schizophrenia, apart from Katrina (mentioned in chapter 5), who had bipolar disorder and was recovering from drug-induced psychosis. Another member of the group was Tamara (also mentioned in chapter 5). They all responded with enthusiasm to the story. Themes were discussed and individuals chose which of the characters they felt most connected to. The three-week process then culminated in a full dramatic enactment using the mini-script. Clients took turns to play the different roles; when they were not acting, they created sound effects or helped to direct one another. It was the interactive group experience that seemed to be the most significant part of the three-week process. Katrina, for example, was new to the unit at this stage. She shared that the Dramatherapy group and story work helped her to feel less lonely and more connected to her new peers.

References

Cartwright M (2018) 'Yin and Yang'. *Ancient History Encyclopaedia Limited.* Available at: https://www.ancient.eu/Yin_and_Yang/

Jung CG (1968) *The Archetypes and the Collective Unconscious* (2nd edition) (Kindle edition). London: Taylor & Francis.

Morris N (2018) *Dramatherapy for Borderline Personality Disorder: Empowering and Nurturing People through Creativity.* London and New York: Routledge.

Richardson D (2017) *Esperanto: Learning and Using the International Language* (4th edition). CreateSpace Independent Publishing Platform.

Stevens A (2001) *Jung: A Very Short Introduction* (Kindle edition). Oxford: Oxford University Press.

Story 9

Survivors

Inner Strength and Courage

Illustration by Nicky Morris

Introduction

Survivors is set in a garden that offers protection to creatures hiding from the outside world. Here, they rebuild their confidence and find the inner strength and courage they need to continue their lives. The idea is that by connecting to these attributes, individuals can allow themselves to be visible, despite the trauma (or any other type of challenging life experience) they have endured. The garden may represent either an internal or physical place and the challenge is to take refuge when needed and then know how and when to step outside. There are five characters in the story: Survivor (a neglected cat), Daring (a brave field mouse), Invisible (a soulful deer), Hope (a hopeful rabbit) and Lively (a mistreated dog). Please note, however, that extra roles may be added, if found through discussion or any of the creative activities described later in the chapter.

Developing the ability to imagine oneself in a safe place is a skill that can help people to cope during particularly stressful times. Mindfulness and visualisation can aid the process and it is used in therapeutic approaches such as Dramatherapy, hypnotherapy and DBT (dialectical behaviour therapy). DBT was developed for people with BPD (borderline personality disorder), also known as EUPD (emotionally unstable personality disorder). In DBT, imagining oneself in a safe space is given as an example of using 'Imagery', the first of the seven components of 'Improving the Moment' – one of the four basic distress tolerance techniques (Linehan, 2015, p446). Clients are encouraged to imagine themselves in a more positive situation, such as entering a safe space: 'Imagine very relaxing scenes of a calming, safe place. Imagine things going well; imagine coping well. Imagine painful emotions draining out of you like water from a tap' (Rathus and Miller, 2014, p289).

Before sharing the story with a group, you could invite your clients or students to imagine that they are in a safe and beautiful garden. Ask them to choose a place to settle. If in a studio space, they can do this actively, using simple props or material if available. Otherwise, visualisation alone can be used. Finally, invite each person to describe their garden and their chosen place within it. Following this, share the story.

Survivors (narrative)[9]

A black cat with white paws padded softly through the snow. Determined to find something to eat, she persevered, as the snowflakes settled on her patchy fur. As the hours passed, she grew so tired that her legs began to weaken. Malnourished and despondent, she curled up in the snow, shivering as the icy wind engulfed her. Seeing that she was in need, a tiny field mouse bravely danced before her, enticing her into a chase. Unable to resist, she stumbled to her feet and the mouse raced ahead. She followed eagerly, her feline instincts reviving her. He ran down a winding alleyway and as they reached its end, she readied herself to pounce. She then watched in dismay as her prey slipped under a wooden gate. Reaching up with a delicate white paw, she pushed against the gate, then nudged it open with her nose.

She found herself in a beautiful walled garden. Fallen branches and tree hollows offered protection from the snow and a freshwater stream flowed, amidst an

---
* The text of this story can be downloaded and printed at www.pavpub.com/find-your-way-resources

abundance of winter berries and foliage. She cautiously began to explore her new surroundings and was astounded to see a gathering of animals, of all shapes and sizes. The field mouse she had chased sat proudly among foxes, rabbits, hedgehogs, deer and squirrels: predators and prey, side by side. The group welcomed her and she tentatively joined them. A young deer with fiery eyes spoke softly to them. Her name was Invisible, which she explained was how she often felt and sometimes wished to be. Her body was scarred, her features delicate, and although she preferred to be alone, she spent a little time with the others each day. She reminded them that the garden was open to any creature in need; the gate would never be locked and they could come and go as they pleased. She also encouraged them to guide others who needed support and shelter to the garden.

The black and white cat was astonished by what she heard and felt deeply grateful for the refuge offered. Each creature then moved towards its own special place in the garden and she watched Invisible disappear into the long grass. Daring, the field mouse, and a rabbit named Hope relaxed among clusters of flowers, while others took shade under the vines and a few leaned against tree roots. They settled wherever they felt safe, as the garden was a sanctuary, hidden from the world outside and away from the people or experiences that had caused them harm or made them afraid.

As winter turned gracefully into spring, the black and white cat elegantly stalked the boundaries of the garden, willing her strength to build. She had adopted the name Survivor. When the animals gathered together, they shared their memories of the world outside and discussed how to avoid the dangers lurking in the shadows. Out there, it wasn't always clear who to trust. Survivor thought it was best not to trust anyone, while Hope believed they might still find genuine friends and a place to belong. To survive, however, they all agreed that courage and determination were essential.

One morning, Survivor heard whimpering and noticed a scruffy young dog cowering in the shadows. His hair was matted, his fringe covering sad, expressive eyes. She had no love for dogs and instinctively her back arched, coat bristled and tail puffed. She then laughed and began to relax, as she remembered her unexpected saviour, Daring. She thought of how brave he had been to help her. Hope told the group that for most of his life the dog had been locked away in the dark, thrown scraps from time to time. He had never known what to expect: food, water or the thump of a stick. Hours earlier, she had burrowed her way into his shed, creating an escape tunnel. She had waited patiently and, when he finally emerged from the darkness, had enticed him into a chase that led him to the garden. Survivor looked again at the frightened young dog and beckoned to him. He crept cautiously out of the shadows.

As spring flowered into summer, the dog grew braver. Each day he spent in the garden, he ventured a little further out of the shadows. Gradually, he learned to enjoy the smell of the earth, barking at the birds that flew in and out of the sanctuary and rolling on the warm grass. The others named him Lively. Invisible watched him with pleasure, though remained out of sight. She saw too that Survivor was stronger now, in body and in spirit. Sensing she may be ready to leave the garden, to seek the freedom and independence she truly wanted, she nudged the gate open for her. She then walked away and lay down by the rose bush. She had grown weary and knew that while others would leave, she would remain. The animals gathered around her, some nuzzling her neck. Although her eyes remained closed, she felt their warmth and their love. She no longer felt invisible.

Survivor moved away from the group and stood tentatively on the threshold between the garden and the outside world. She remained poised, ready to leap towards a new life. Lively watched her, his tail wagging. He considered following her, knowing that he was also free to leave. He was afraid of returning to the dark, however, and did not know if he was ready. Survivor looked back fondly at the beautiful garden and her new friends. Invisible had once told them that there was a place for each of them, both inside and outside the garden. She had also said that the garden was a place to rest, rather than remain.

The story pauses here.

Survivor is on the verge of leaving the garden and Lively is watching her, considering his future. What do you think they will do next and how would you like their story to end?

Creative activities

Several activities can be offered in relation to *Survivors* and new activities may also be created. The list below describes key exercises that have been used successfully with groups and some can be adapted for individual work. You do not have to introduce every activity, nor follow the order in which they are listed. Discussion, however, is often an effective way to begin. The energy or nature of a group – or an individual's initial response to the story – will also guide you towards the most appropriate and effective way of working with it. Some people enjoy participating in script work for example, while others may prefer the freedom of improvisation. On the other hand, you might have selected this story in order to steer your students or clients in a specific direction – to encourage creative writing, for example. There is no right or wrong way to work with the story, just as there is no right or wrong choice for Survivor or Lively to make.

Discussion and choices

After sharing Survivors, encourage your students or clients to discuss what they thought about the story and to choose which of the animals they feel most connected to. Each person can also choose a line in the story (about their chosen animal, perhaps) that makes the most impact on them. If there are more than six participants, splitting into pairs or smaller groups may be useful.

Questions to consider:

- ▶ To which character in the story do you feel most connected and why?
- ▶ How do you think the story should end?
- ▶ Will Survivor leave the garden?

- ▶ If Survivor leaves the garden, will Lively follow?
- ▶ We know why Survivor and Lively are introduced to the garden. What might have drawn Daring (the field mouse), Hope (the rabbit) and Invisible (the deer) there initially?
- ▶ Why do you think that Daring (the field mouse) and Hope (the rabbit) continue to live in the garden, when they appear confident enough to remain outside its walls?

After these discussions, bring the group back together and invite everyone to share their thoughts. If working in pairs, one approach is to ask each member to say what their partner decided and why. If working with an individual, adapt the process accordingly. It is again important to remember that the choices people make at this point are likely to reflect something significant about their current mood and mental state, or even about their memories.

Imagine your own garden

Invite your students or clients to imagine that they are each animals, taking refuge in a safe and beautiful garden. Visualisation can be used and the following questions explored:

1. What type of animal are you? (Consider physical description and personality traits.)
2. Did another animal lead you to the garden?
3. What does the garden look like?
4. Where would you settle in the garden?
5. Who or what do you need time away from?
6. What would you like to gain from your time in the garden?
7. Are you ready to leave the garden or do you want to stay longer?

Artwork

Invite your students or clients to create a piece of artwork in response to the story, using whatever art and craft materials are available. You could offer the following options:

A. Ask people to consider how they would imagine their own garden of sanctuary to look – a place to take refuge and receive support. (They may have explored this during an earlier activity.) They can then create a piece of artwork (2D or 3D) to represent their garden. This could also be a group activity, with several people creating a garden together.

B. Create a piece of artwork (2D or 3D) to symbolise any animal they would like to be.

C. Alternatively, create a piece of artwork (2D or 3D) to symbolise:

   a. Their favourite character from the story.
   b. A significant theme from the story.
   c. A chosen moment from the story.

Story 9: Survivors

If working with a group, encourage your clients or students to show one another their artwork when ready, as sharing and witnessing each other's creations is an important part of the process. This activity is appropriate for both group and individual work.

Creative writing

A helpful strategy to introduce creative writing is to ask an individual (or members of a group) to imagine what would happen if the story were to continue. There are several possibilities and the questions listed in both the 'Discussion and Choices' and 'Imagine Your Own Garden' section may be helpful. Participants could:

1. Continue to write the narrative version of the story.
2. Continue to write the mini script that follows.
3. Write a monologue for one (or more) of the five characters. This can focus on the events described in the story, what happened to them previously or whatever happens next.
4. Write a short story about a new animal character, who takes refuge in the garden. A monologue (in the first person) could also be written. Consider the following questions as a guide:
    a. What type of animal is it? (Include physical description and personality traits.)
    b. Which animal led him or her to the garden?
    c. Who or what do they need time away from?
    d. How long have they been in the garden?
    e. Do they interact with the other animals or spend more time alone?
    f. What are they hoping to gain from their time in the garden?
    g. Do they want to stay in the garden or do they feel ready to leave?

Hot seating and improvisation

Survivors has a lot of scope for both character work and dramatic enactment through hot seating, roleplay and improvisation. Although five roles are indicated, characters can be shared, added or omitted, to adapt to each group's needs. The questions listed in both the 'Discussion and Choices' and 'Imagine Your Own Garden' sections could be useful. Roleplay and hot seating (or interviewing) are techniques that can help people to explore characters further – identifying their strengths, weaknesses, hopes and fears, etc. Hot seating involves each member of the group taking turns to imagine themselves in a chosen role, while their peers ask them questions. Roleplay, however, is a more fluid process, during which people may improvise a scene together in character.

The following dramatic exercises could be offered:

1. Create a montage of tableaus, symbolising key moments identified in the narrative.
2. Use hot seating to further explore the five characters in the story.
3. Improvise mini scenes to dramatise key moments identified in the narrative.
4. Continue the story from the moment the narrative ends, with improvisation.

A personalised version of the hot seating and improvisation process can also be used:

5. Use hot seating to explore newly imagined characters for the story – questions can include:
   a. What type of animal are you? (Consider physical description and personality traits.)
   b. Did another animal lead you to the garden?
   c. How long have you been there?
   d. Who or what do you need time away from?
   e. Do you interact with the other animals or spend more time alone?
   f. What would you like to gain from your time in the garden?
   g. Do you want to stay in the garden or do you feel ready to leave?

6. Using improvisation, create a new story (or scene) with the new characters found through the hot seating activity, or previous discussions, or creative writing, etc.

Survivors (mini script)

The mini script has three short scenes. There are five characters included (although non-speaking animal characters could be added). With a large group, smaller groups could form, each being given a different scene to work on, for example. If available, simple props and/or masks could be used, as well as director and designer roles. The words in italics are suggested stage directions.

Survivor:	A determined black and white cat
Daring:	A courageous, cheeky little field mouse
Invisible:	A gentle deer, protector of the garden
Hope:	A brave and cheerful rabbit
Lively:	A nervous, scruffy young dog
Extras:	Any chosen animal
Scene 1	4 characters – Survivor, Daring, Invisible and Hope
Survivor:	I need something to eat and I'm so thirsty, but it's freezing and my legs ache. I can't carry on like this, I need to rest. It's hopeless. *(She curls up in the snow and closes her eyes)*
Daring:	Wake up! Wake up! Come on, cat. Follow me.
Survivor:	Crazy little mouse. *(Struggles to her feet)*

Story 9: Survivors

Daring:	Catch me if you can! *(Runs towards the garden gate)*
Survivor:	You're mine! *(Chases the mouse)*
Daring:	Follow me if you dare… *(Slips under the garden gate)*
Survivor:	Where did you go? Pesky mouse. I'm coming for you. *(Pushes the gate open)*
Invisible:	Welcome to our garden, cat. My name is Invisible.
Survivor:	That's a strange name.
Invisible:	It's how I often feel and sometimes wish to be.
Daring:	Predators and prey live side by side here.
Survivor:	What if I don't want to live here?
Invisible:	The gate is never locked. You're free to come and go as you please.
Hope:	Don't be afraid, cat.
Daring:	I led you here for a reason.
Invisible:	The garden is for any creature in need of support.
Hope:	You can shelter from the snow, eat berries and drink fresh water.
Invisible:	The garden will protect you; it's a sanctuary.
Survivor:	Thank you. *(Survivor and each of the animals settle in their own special place in the garden)*
Scene 2	5 characters – Survivor, Daring, Invisible, Hope and Lively
Invisible:	Winter has turned into spring.
Daring:	Yet danger still lurks in the shadows outside.
Survivor:	I'm not afraid – the snow has melted and the sun is shining.
Daring:	I've seen you sunbathing.
Survivor:	Very funny, Daring. I also walk, run and climb every day.
Hope:	You're so much stronger now.
Invisible:	Are you thinking of leaving us, Survivor?
Survivor:	Not yet, but I would like to join the outside world again soon.
Daring:	It's not always clear who to trust out there.

Story 9: Survivors

Survivor:	Then I'll trust no one.
Invisible:	Courage and determination are all you need, Survivor.
Hope:	And there may be genuine friends to be found.
Invisible:	Whatever you decide, there will always be a place for you in the garden.
Lively:	*(Whimpers – cowering in the shadows)*
Hope:	I forgot to say … we have a new arrival, a scruffy young dog.
Survivor:	I hate dogs!
Hope:	He's frightened. See, he's hiding in the shadows.
Daring:	Things are different in the garden, remember?
Survivor:	I remember.
Lively:	*(Whimpers again)*
Invisible:	Come out, little dog.
Daring:	Come on, you're safe here.
Hope:	I found him locked in a shed. Most of his life, he was kept in the dark, thrown scraps from time to time.
Daring:	Poor little mutt.
Hope:	He never knew what to expect: food, water or the thump of a stick.
Survivor:	It's okay, little dog. My name is Survivor. In the winter, I was scared and weak, just like you.
Hope:	And now she's strong and confident.
Survivor:	The animals here will help you.
Lively:	Are you sure? *(Cautiously steps out of the shadows)*
Hope:	That's why I led you here.
Survivor:	The garden is a sanctuary.
Invisible:	You will find shelter from the sun, berries to eat and fresh water to drink.
Lively:	Thank you.
Scene 3	5 characters – Survivor, Daring, Invisible, Hope and Lively
Daring:	Spring has turned into summer.

Story 9: Survivors

Hope:	The garden looks beautiful.
Survivor:	And just look at Lively!
Hope:	He's learning to play, sniffing the earth, barking at birds and rolling in the grass.
Survivor:	Yes, he's becoming a true dog.
Daring:	You'd better watch out, then!
Survivor:	Very funny, Daring.
Hope:	Where's Invisible?
Daring:	She's been spending more time alone, watching us from the shadows.
Survivor:	She seems so tired.
Daring:	I'm worried about her.
Hope:	Come and join us, Lively, don't be afraid.
Daring:	Have you seen Invisible today?
Lively:	Yes, I saw her by the gate.
Survivor:	Did she speak to you?
Lively:	Yes, but her voice was very soft. She said she was happy to see me playing.
Daring:	Anything else?
Lively:	She nudged the gate open and said that Survivor was confident and strong now, so might want to leave.
Survivor:	What did she do after that, Lively?
Lively:	She walked away slowly and lay down by the rose bush.
Hope:	Let's go to her. *(The animals gather around Invisible)*
Daring:	We're all here, Invisible.
Hope:	You can rest now.
Invisible:	*(Her eyes remain closed, but she speaks softly)* ... No longer invisible.
Survivor:	*(Leaves the group with Invisible and moves towards the open gate).*
Lively:	*(Watches Survivor and follows her to the gate)*

Lively:	What are you doing, Survivor?
Survivor:	I think it may be time for me to leave.
Lively:	Will you come back?
Survivor:	Maybe. Remember, the garden is a place to rest, not to remain. We can come and go as we please.
Lively:	I remember. Can I come too?
Survivor:	Are you ready to leave?
Lively:	I'm not sure.
Survivor:	Are you still afraid of the dark?
Lively:	Yes.
Survivor:	Look after yourself, little dog.

The story pauses here…

Survivor is on the verge of leaving the garden and Lively is watching her, considering his future.

What do you think they will do next and how would you like their story to end?

Examples of work in practice

You may discover that, while some people enjoy having a copy of the story to follow, others prefer to relax and listen. Likewise, some might respond well to script work and others will favour a freer, more spontaneous approach. As reflective discussions develop among one group, another will choose to remain in the creative realm. Choice is the prevailing element here, just as in *Survivors*, where Survivor and Lively are free to decide what to do at the end of the story. It is imperative that everyone is heard and their choices respected. In a group this could prove challenging at times and as a facilitator one should try to be as flexible as possible, while encouraging compromise and finding the most appropriate method with which to proceed.

One following poignant example follows, in which pseudonyms are used:

Personal Connections – Young women with EUPD

Survivors was inspired by Bethany, a young woman in her early 20s, who I met and worked with on the female low secure ward for EUPD (introduced in chapter 1). She enjoyed exploring the stories in this collection, loved to sing and felt a deep affinity with animals. She also struggled with intense suicidal urges and dissociated between different states of being. I began to write *Survivors* whilst working with Bethany. She once described her ability to imagine herself in a magical garden when reality became too stressful for her. Childhood trauma continued to haunt her, however, and despite her valiant efforts to move towards recovery, she tragically committed suicide. I found it difficult to complete the story, though did so eventually, and the character Invisible is closely related to Bethany.

Several months after her death, I introduced *Survivors* to a small group of young women on the ward. Before sharing the story, I invited them to move around the space and to imagine themselves in a safe and beautiful garden. They were encouraged to picture how the garden would look and were asked to find a place in the garden to settle. After this, each of them was given the opportunity to describe the garden they had imagined and the place they had chosen to rest. The story was then shared and they were asked to consider which of the five characters they felt most connected to.

1. **Roxanne** (mentioned in chapter 7) had been close friends with Bethany and was now struggling with grief. She chose the character of Lively, in relation to his past rather than his present. She explained that she felt as though she was trapped in the dark, just as Lively had been physically locked in a shed.

2. **Peggy** was new to the ward and this was the first story she had encountered. She selected the character of Survivor and said she liked cats. At the end of the session, however, she reflected that she had somehow prevented herself from connecting too deeply to the process and felt that others had responded more openly. She was reassured that there was no right or wrong way to respond to a story (or any Dramatherapy activity) and that it takes time to build confidence and trust. Interestingly, this is also an important aspect of Survivor's journey in the story.

3. **Betty** responded sensitively to *Survivors*. She felt a strong connection to the character of Invisible, explaining that she often wished she could be unseen. She said, however, that she also hoped to become more like Survivor, developing both physical and emotional strength.

References

Linehan MM (2015) *DBT Skills Training Manual* (2nd edition). New York: The Guilford Press.

Rathus JH & Miller AL (2015) *DBT Skills Manual for Adolescents*. New York: The Guilford Press.

Story 10

Nature's Spirits

Environmental Issues, Personality Types and Choice

Illustration by Nicky Morris

Story 10: Nature's Spirits

Introduction

Nature's Spirits encourages people to explore and express their individuality, while also considering themselves in relation to the world at large. Current environmental issues, including global warming, deforestation and pollution, are gently introduced, as the story follows a group of young nature spirits, who must leave the protective embrace of Aether, the wise and spiritual, to travel across the ancient, elemental realms of Earth, Fire, Water and Air. This final story mirrors aspects of the first story in the collection, *The Glow Fish*. At the end of the story, the young spirits remember Aether's advice, that they must each find their own way. These words are found in the collection's title and encapsulate a theme that flows through all ten stories.

Through metaphor, *Nature's Spirits* encourages people to consider the current state of our planet and what part they might choose to play in contributing to positive change. Climate change is a serious issue that young people are striving to address. In January 2019, Greta Thunberg, a 16-year-old Swedish activist, spoke passionately at the World Economic Forum in Davos about climate change and the impact it will have on future generations. She accused the world leaders present of serious negligence and her speech went viral, inspiring millions of young people across the world to act (Hitchings-Hale, 2019). Huge rallies have since taken place across every continent and, on 20 September 2019, more than 7.6 million people took part in a week of global climate strikes:

'millions of students, parents, trade unions, businesses, health workers, scientists, celebrities, people of all backgrounds, ages, regions and faiths came together in all corners of the globe calling for climate action. More than 6,100 events were held in 185 countries, with the support of 73 Trade Unions, 820 civil society organizations, 3,000 companies and 8,500 websites.' (Global Climate Strike, 2019)

Nature's Spirits also offers an exploration of personality types, structured around the properties of the ancient elements, Earth, Fire, Water and Air:

Earth is grounding and symbolises prosperity, fertility, stability, orderliness, sustenance, creativity, physical abundance, nourishment, solidity, dependability, security, permanence, intuition, introspection and wisdom (Ancient Symbols, 2019).

Fire connects to transformational and purifying powers. It symbolises energy, activity, creativity, passion, freedom, power, love, vision, anger, strength, will, assertiveness, courage and dynamism. Whilst fire offers warmth and enables life, it can also burn and destroy (Ancient Symbols, 2019).

Water symbolises dreaming, healing, flowing, fluidity, purification, regeneration, stability, strength, change, fertility, devotion and unconditional love. It also symbolises both death and rebirth. Whilst life giving, it can be formidable and destructive (Ancient Symbols, 2019).

Air is the breath of life, clear and cleansing. It symbolises communication, intelligence, perception, knowledge, learning, thinking, imagination, creativity, harmony and travel. At times, air can also become a force of terrible destruction (Ancient Symbols, 2019).

In the fifth century BCE, the Greek philosopher Empedocles revealed that all natural phenomena could be explained by the interaction between the four elements and their relationship with the forces of love and strife (Drako, 2018, pp2–3). Aristotle then developed these ideas further and introduced the concept of Spirit (or Aether), which became known as the fifth element (Lipp, 2004, pp15–16). Hippocrates went on to connect the nature of the elements to four personality types and viewed them as bodily fluids or 'humours' (Marks, 1998). The four elements were believed to exist within people as well as nature, as the two interrelate. Influenced by these theories, many philosophers and alchemists then considered the importance of maintaining a healthy balance between the four elements, to support both physical and psychological well-being. Science and medicine have of course evolved considerably since then, and the modern periodic table describes over a hundred complex elements, for example. Despite this, Empedocles' original ideas have influenced many traditions (including astrology and Jungian psychology) and remain relevant to modern society, from both a spiritual and psychological perspective.

Finally, the work of Paracelsus should be noted. A radical physician, alchemist and philosopher of the 16th century, he challenged many of the medical and religious practices of the time and established the role of chemistry in medicine (Hargarve, 2019). He also wrote many books, including *Nymphs, Sylphs, Pygmies and Salamanders*, in which he introduced the elemental spirits who take care of the planet's elements: Nymphs were the water spirits; Sylphs the air spirits; Pygmies the earth spirits; and Salamanders the fire spirits (Ball, 2006, p318).

Nature's Spirits (narrative)[10]

The Earth Queen rumbled, struggling to sustain balance, as more of her forests were annihilated.

The Fire King roared, as he stoked his embers and unleashed his flames.

The Water Queen screamed, for her oceans were polluted, her icebergs melting too fast.

The Air King moaned, choking on the toxins swirling through his skies.

And Aether, the wise and spiritual, wept, moving in between them, longing for meaning.

The human world was in chaos, struggling to maintain balance and to contain its power over the elements. Nature's spirits were confronted with a daunting future and overwhelmed by the challenge, many no longer wanted to remain in their separate realms. Their royal leaders encouraged loyalty and perseverance however, while desperately seeking newly born nature spirits to join them. Conflicting beliefs and opinions spread across the elemental realms, mirroring the essence of the human world. Both were in jeopardy.

---
* The text of this story can be downloaded and printed at www.pavpub.com/find-your-way-resources

Story 10: Nature's Spirits

Aether, the wise and spiritual, prepared a group of nature's young spirits, to leave her protective embrace. They were to travel across the four elemental realms of Earth, Fire, Water and Air. Each realm was unique, yet all were connected and equally powerful. Aether said they must explore every realm, as the journey would help them to learn about themselves and one another. Only then could they help to bring balance back to the world. They felt both excited by and fearful of the challenges ahead.

The four realms possessed contrasting forces of energy, both physical and emotional. As they struggled to decide which to explore first, the ground beneath them began to rumble and the Earth Queen rose up before them.

'Greetings, young nature spirits. There's nothing to fear. I am the Earth Queen. I am wise and dependable, grounded and stable, creative and intuitive. Join me on the land and find your roots. Lie among the budding flowers and feel the earth breathe beneath you. Then help me to regain balance across the earth and nurture new tree seedlings. Together, we will bind fire, water and air.'

The young spirits listened intently, then did as she asked. They lay together on the earth, amongst the young trees and budding flowers, then stared up at the wide sky above. They felt no need to move, until the sun appeared to suddenly explode. Vibrant streaks of orange and red cascaded around them and they were submerged in an intense heat. From the roar of the flames, the Fire King appeared.

'Wake up, young spirits. I am the Fire King. Come and help me to unleash the power and potential of my beautiful flames. I am brave and free, passionate and dynamic, sometimes angry and destructive, yet vibrant and loving. Warm yourselves around my fire and stare into the flames. Creativity and electricity will flow through you, opening countless possibilities.'

The young spirits felt both afraid and inspired by his words, then did as he suggested and sat around the fire he had created. As they stared into the swirling flames and allowed the warmth to flow through them, they were abruptly shaken by the sound of a piercing scream, followed by a shower of icy water that put out the fire. The Water Queen glided into sight.

'Hear me, young spirits. I am the Water Queen and I need your help. My oceans are polluted, my glaciers melting too fast. I am strong and devoted, a dreamer and a healer. Sometimes formidable and destructive, yet mostly adaptable and life giving. Come and refresh yourselves in my stream. Allow the cool water to flow over you and embrace the magnetic power of my waters. Then we can purify my oceans.'

The young spirits listened carefully to her words and did as she asked. They stepped into her stream and enjoyed the feel of the clear water flowing over them. They began to splash and play in the water, until a loud moan echoed through the sky and the Air King appeared.

'Come and help me, young spirits. I am the Air King and I'm choking on the toxins filling my skies. I am a creative traveller, perceptive and intelligent. I can be terribly

destructive, yet mostly I bring harmony and clarity. I am the breath of life. Come with me and we can fly together across the earth, purify the air and bring the elements of fire and water together.'

The young spirits listened and did as he suggested. They left the stream and took flight with the Air King, looking down on the world below. They watched as the Earth, Fire, Water and Air spirits danced courageously with the elements. They felt both exhilarated and afraid, realising that each realm had the potential for both pleasure and pain. While they understood themselves a little better, they remained unsure where to settle, so asked the Air King if they could travel between the realms. He shuddered at the suggestion, suggesting it might tear them apart and stressing the importance of loyalty and focus. They bravely considered moving in separate directions, then wondered if they could instead return to Aether. They missed her guidance and then remembered her words: 'You must each find your own way.'

The story pauses here and what happens next is your choice.

Creative activities

Several activities can be offered in relation to *Nature's Spirits* and new activities may also be created. The list below describes key exercises that have been used successfully with groups and some can be adapted for individual work. You do not have to introduce every activity, nor follow the order in which they are listed. Discussion, however, is often an effective way to begin. The energy or nature of a group – or an individual's initial response to the story – will also guide you towards the most appropriate and effective way of working with it. Some people may feel most at ease with creative writing, for example, while others might prefer to express themselves through artwork. On the other hand, you might have selected this story in order to steer your students or clients in a specific direction – to encourage dramatic enactment, for example. There is no right or wrong way to work with the story, just as there is no right or wrong choice for the young nature spirits to make.

Discussion and choices

After sharing *Nature's Spirits*, encourage your students or clients to discuss what they thought about the story and to which of the elemental realms they feel most connected. Each person can also choose a line in the story (about their chosen element, perhaps) that makes the most impact on them. If there are more than six participants, splitting into pairs or smaller groups may be useful.

The following questions could be explored:

▶ To which elemental realm in the story do you feel most connected, and why?

▶ Is there another element that you would like to explore?

▶ How do you think the story should end?

a. Will the young nature spirits each choose a different realm to settle in?

b. Do they have an alternative, such as moving between all four realms?

After these discussions, bring the group back together and invite everyone to share their thoughts. If working in pairs, one approach is to ask each member to say what their partner decided and why. It's also important to remember that the choices people make at this point may reflect something significant about their current mood and mental state, or their memories.

Dramatic tableaus

Each of the four elements symbolises a different personality type (as mentioned in the introduction). Ask your students or clients to choose which of the elemental realms they feel most connected to: Earth, Water, Air or Fire. Then invite them to form mini groups based on their choices. In these groups, participants can work together to create a dramatic tableau (defined as a group of motionless figures representing a scene) symbolising their chosen elemental realm. They can do this using their bodies. Voice can also be used, to add words or sound effects, and the tableaus can be either still or moving. If props are available, a selection of materials (different colours and textures) masks, percussive instruments, etc. could be useful. When ready, the groups should be encouraged to show one another their dramatic tableaus.

Artwork

As described in the exercise above, invite the members of your group to form mini groups based on the choice they made: Earth, Fire, Air or Water. Participants can then work together to create a piece of art/craft work to represent their chosen elemental realm. They can do this using whatever arts, crafts and collage materials are available. When ready, the groups should be encouraged to present their creations to one another. Alternatively, your participants could produce individual pieces of artwork.

Creative writing

Creative writing works equally well with an individual or group. A helpful strategy to introduce it is to ask people to imagine what would happen if the story were to continue. There are several possibilities:

1. Continue to write the narrative version of the story
2. Continue to write the mini script that follows.
3. Focus on a single character's journey, in story or monologue form.

Hot seating and improvisation

Nature's Spirits has a lot of scope for both character work and dramatic enactment through hot seating, roleplay and improvisation. Although nine roles are indicated, characters can be shared, added or omitted to adapt to each group's needs. Roleplay and hot seating (or interviewing) are techniques that can help people to explore characters further – to identify their strengths, weaknesses, hopes and fears, etc. Hot seating involves each member of the group taking turns to imagine themselves in a chosen role, while their peers ask them questions. Roleplay, however, is a more fluid process, during which people may improvise a scene together in character.

The following dramatic exercises could be offered:

1. Create a montage of tableaus, symbolising key moments identified in the narrative.
2. Use hot seating to further explore the characters in the story.
3. Improvise mini scenes to dramatise key moments identified in the narrative.
4. Continue the story from the moment the narrative ends, with improvisation.

Nature's Spirits (mini script)

There are five mini-scenes and potentially nine characters (who can be male or female): four young nature spirits, Aether (the wise and spiritual), the Earth Queen, the Fire King, the Water Queen and the Air King. Roles can interchange and, in a small group, nature spirits 1 and 3 could be read by one person, as could spirits 2 and 4. Larger groups could split into smaller groups of 3 to 5 people, taking one scene each, for example. Director, designer and sound effects roles could also be added and simple props or costume used. Stage directions are suggested in italics.

Scene 1:	Aether and 4 young nature spirits (or 2, if 2/4 and 1/3 are merged).
Nature Spirit 1:	Why are you weeping, Aether?
Aether:	I was moving between Earth, Fire, Water and Air.
Nature Spirit 2:	What happened?
Aether:	I saw their struggles and I long for meaning.
Nature Spirit 3:	Can we help?
Aether:	Listen carefully, young Spirits. Tell me what you hear?
Nature Spirit 4:	The Earth Queen rumbles.
Nature Spirit 1:	The Fire King roars.
Nature Spirit 2:	The Water Queen screams.
Nature Spirit 3:	The Air King moans.
Nature Spirit 4:	What does it mean, Aether?
Aether:	There's unrest across the realms, mirroring the chaos of the human world.

Story 10: Nature's Spirits

Nature Spirit 1:	What should we do?
Aether:	The time has come for you to visit the elemental realms of Earth, Fire, Water and Air.
Nature Spirit 2:	Will you come with us?
Aether:	No, I'm afraid you must each find your own way.
Nature Spirit 3:	I'm not sure we're ready.
Aether:	Don't worry. The journey will help you to learn more about yourselves. Seek balance and you will find meaning.
Nature Spirit 4:	Where should we begin?
Aether:	Trust in the elements, they will guide you. Goodbye, young spirits, and good luck.
Scene 2:	The Earth Queen and 4 young nature spirits (or 2, if 2/4 and 1/3 are merged).
Nature Spirit 1:	We're alone.
Nature Spirit 2:	I'm afraid.
Nature Spirit 3:	Me too. *(The young nature spirits then hear a loud rumbling sound)*
Earth Queen:	Greetings, young nature spirits. There's nothing to fear. I am the Earth Queen. I'm wise and dependable, grounded and stable, creative and intuitive. Join me on the land and find your roots.
Nature Spirit 4:	How do we do that?
Earth Queen:	Lie among the budding flowers and feel the earth breathe beneath you. *(The young nature spirits do as she asks and lie on the earth)*
Nature Spirit 1:	I feel calm and safe.
Earth Queen:	Then help me to regain balance across the earth and nurture new tree seedlings. Together, we will bind fire, water and air.
Scene 3:	The Fire King and 4 young nature spirits (or 2, if 2/4 and 1/3 are merged). *(While lying on the earth, among the flowers, the young nature spirits are alarmed to hear a loud roaring sound)*
Nature Spirit 2:	What's happening?

Nature Spirit 3:	I'm frightened.
Nature Spirit 4:	It's so hot.
Fire King:	Wake up, young spirits. I am the Fire King. I am brave and free, passionate and dynamic, sometimes angry and destructive, yet vibrant and loving.
Nature Spirit 1:	What do you want from us?
Fire King:	Come and help me to unleash the power and potential of my beautiful flames.
Nature Spirit 4:	How do we do that?
Fire King:	Warm yourselves around my fire, stare into the flames. Creativity and electricity will flow through you, opening countless possibilities. *(The young nature spirits do as he asks and sit around the fire)*
Nature Spirit 2:	I feel alive!
Nature Spirit 3:	It's both daunting and inspiring.
Scene 4:	The Water Queen and 4 young nature spirits (or 2, if 2/4 and 1/3 are merged). *(While sitting around the fire, the young nature spirits are shocked to hear a piercing scream)*
Water Queen:	Hear me, young nature spirits, I am the Water Queen and I need your help. My oceans are polluted, my glaciers melting too fast.
Nature Spirit 4:	That's terrible.
Water Queen:	I'm strong and devoted, a dreamer and a healer. Sometimes formidable and destructive, yet mostly adaptable and life giving.
Nature Spirit 1:	What can we do?
Water Queen:	Come and refresh yourselves in my stream. Allow the cool water to purify your senses. Then embrace the magnetic power of my waters and together, we can purify my oceans. Healing. *(The young nature spirits do as she asks and splash around in the stream)*
Nature Spirit 2:	It's soothing,
Nature Spirit 1:	And invigorating.

Story 10: Nature's Spirits

Scene 5:	The Earth Queen and 4 young nature spirits (or 2, if 2/4 and 1/3 are merged). *(The young nature spirits are splashing in the stream, then stop when they hear a loud moan)*
Nature Spirit 3:	Who's there?
Air King:	It is I, the Air King. Come and help me, young spirits. I'm choking on the toxins filling my skies.
Nature Spirit 4:	How are you coping?
Air King:	I am the breath of life, a creative traveller, perceptive and intelligent. I can be terribly destructive, yet mostly I bring harmony and clarity.
Nature Spirit 1:	What can we do?
Air King:	Come with me and we can fly together across the earth, purify the air and bring the elements of fire and water together. *(The young nature spirits do as he asks, leave the stream and take flight)*
Nature Spirit 2:	I feel weightless and free.
Nature Spirit 1:	I can see more clearly.
Air King:	What do you see?
Nature Spirit 3:	All the nature spirits, dancing courageously with the elements.
Nature Spirit 4:	Every realm, showing the potential for both pleasure and pain.
Air King:	How do you feel?
Nature Spirit 1:	Exhilarated.
Nature Spirit 2:	Afraid.
Nature Spirit 3:	I understand myself a little better.
Air King:	So, young spirits, will you stay with me?
Nature Spirit 4:	I'm not sure.
Nature Spirit 1:	Can we not travel between the realms?
Air King:	It could tear you apart and I need loyalty and focus.
Nature Spirit 2:	What should we do?
Nature Spirit 3:	I miss Aether.
Nature Spirit 4:	Me too.
Nature Spirit 1:	Maybe we can return to her?

Air King:	What did she tell you?
Nature Spirit 2:	That we must each find our own way.

Examples of work in practice

Team building with mental health professionals

I introduced *Nature's Spirits* as part of a team building day organised for my colleagues on the secure ward for women with EUPD (described in chapter 1). It was an interactive experience which led to spontaneous improvisation during the storytelling, and I used a few simple props to enhance the experience. My intention was to bring the team together with a fun yet thought provoking activity. It also offered insight into the work I do with our service users, while encouraging communication, confidence and self-expression among my peers. As the APPGAHW (All-Party Parliamentary Group on Arts, Health and Wellbeing) reveals, 'Cultural engagement and arts therapy can improve wellbeing in healthcare staff' (2017b, p1). Before telling the story, I invited colleagues to volunteer to read the parts of the four royal spirits. Ebenezer, an RMN (registered mental health nurse), who I have worked with for several years, agreed to be the Air King. He wrote the following in response to the experience.

'I'm Ebenezer Quaye, an RMN (Registered Mental Health Nurse) on a secure ward for women with EUPD. I attended a team building day in July 2019 and participated in a story workshop run by Nicky, our dramatherapist. The story was called "Nature's Spirits". I was given the opportunity to read out the part of the Air King. It was a bit difficult to begin with, as I was not expecting to read out loud in front of my peers, but I was able to gather the courage and to accept the challenge. After reading the story, we were asked to move into separate groups, depending on which of the four spirits we felt most connected to. I chose to be part of the Air King's group. We all agreed that air was the most important element, because without it, we cannot live or survive on this Earth. Oxygen and life support are used to help people who cannot breathe on their own. It is paramount to our existence. We then created a dramatic tableau with sound and movement, to symbolise the element of Air.

The story workshop helped to bring awareness to people, encouraging us to understand the important elements of life. Seeing my peers taking part gave me a sense of belonging and I then took this experience with me into my day to day work.'

References

Ancient Symbols (2019) Four Elements Symbolism. *Ancient Symbols website*. Available at: https://www.ancient-symbols.com/four-elements.html

All-Party Parliamentary Group on Arts, Health and Wellbeing – APPGAHW (2017) *Creative Health: The Arts for Health and Wellbeing – Inquiry Report* (2nd edition). London: All-Party Parliamentary Group on Arts, Health and Wellbeing. Available at: https://www.culturehealthandwellbeing.org.uk/appg-inquiry/

Ball P (2006) *The Devil's Doctor: Paracelsus and the World of Renaissance Magic and Science*. London: William Heinemann.

Draco M (2018) *Pagan Portals – The Power of the Elements: The Magical Approach to Earth, Air, Fire, Water & Spirit*. New Alresford: Moon Books.

Global Climate Strikes (2019) 7.6 million people demand action after week of climate strikes. *Global Climate Strike Website*. Available at: https://globalclimatestrike.net/7-million-people-demand-action-after-week-of-climate-strikes/

Hargarve J (2019) Paracelsus. *Encyclopaedia Britannica website*. Available at: https://www.britannica.com/science/surgery-medicine

Hitchings-Hales J (2019) 'Thousands of British Students Will Join Friday's Global School Walkout against Climate Change'. *Global Citizen*. Available at: https://www.globalcitizen.org/en/content/british-students-climate-change-protest-school-/

Lipp D (2004) *The Way of Four: Create Elemental Balance in Your Life*. St. Paul: Llewellyn Publications.

Marks T (1998) Elemental: The Four Elements. From Ancient Greek Science and Philosophy to Poetry. *Webwinds website*. Available at: http://www.webwinds.com/thalassa/elemental.htm

Quaye E (2019) Email with feedback on 'Nature's Spirits', in relation to this publication.

Appendix

Response to – Boy in a Tree

I read a story about a young man who retreated to the trees.
I felt I partially understood him,
And maybe him me.
He observed the world from a safe distance.
From somewhere his mum could see,
That he was ok and held by the branches and peace of the canopy.

He saw a young woman;
It could easily have been me.
Escaping the chaos of life and trying to learn how to be.
She wished to not be alone, but for a ceasing of confusion and for friends without words.
She was merely surviving and cornered by expectations.
Forced to her own tree to gain a sense of ease.
Not respected for this by family or friends,
But constantly forced to return to a world that made no sense and drove her insane.

Moments of ecstasy fleetingly existed for both the young man and woman.
A 'conversation', with the squirrel.
A paddle in the refreshing stream that sang its own song.
And eventually a glimpse of others in the trees and knowing they were not alone.

The women almost wished for corporate isolation.
For all to see that her fear to be and to not be,
Were not an unusual way of being.
That time to reflect, refresh and re-root is needed by us all.
How long and regular that time required is different for us all.

Soon corporate isolation was forced upon us all.
The woman felt guilty at first,
For wishing for this to be,
But she recognised her and the young man's relief at this solidarity.
And realised that these new expectations were an opportunity for many to find their tree.
A chance to discover who they are and why they might need a canopy in which to retreat.
It promoted an understanding that although alone,
We are still part of the world.
And, we are all braver than we think.

Appendix

This time will pass and many will leave their trees for good.
I wish they would remember their way back.
But they won't and expectations will weigh heavy and they will forget their need.
Not just that,
But the needs of others to.
The need to retreat to the canopy and observe a confusing world and just be.
The young man and woman will be forced to survive and not to thrive.
Solidarity will be lost and confusion and expectations will reign,
With needs ignored and individual's ecstasy snubbed,
Left trampled on the floor.

We have time the young women thought.
This wasn't the corporate isolation I had hoped and wished for.
But we have time and plenty of trees to climb.
And at a safe distance to see;
That there is solidarity in seeking out your tree.
And you're braver than you know if you take the time to do this when a pandemic isn't in full flow.

The young man and woman clapped,
As they observed so many in the confusing world ascending their tree and feeling the bravery that it took.
And so, they shouted at the top of their voice.
"Silent solidarity can be found in these trees."
"You are not alone,
And change is possible."
"Things may not be as bad as they seem."
And in a whisper from their Oak and Cedar;
They said "…and maybe now you'll understand and pass by with a glance and a smile.
Not trying to force us down.
Instead giving us the gift of time.
And not forgetting your tree still stands."

Camilla Bartrop
29/03/2020

Childhood TRAUMA and Recovery

A Child-Centred Approach to Healing Early Years Abuse

Mary Walsh and Neil Thompson

Mary Walsh and Neil Thompson

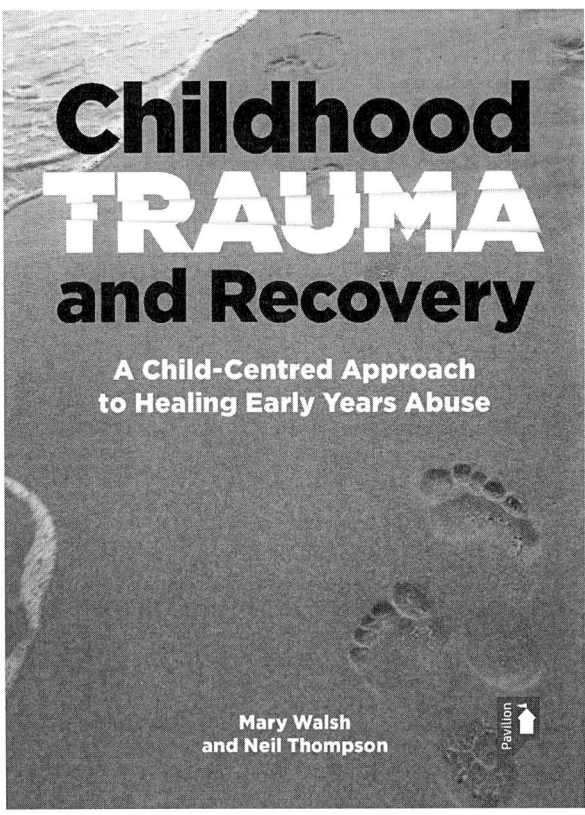

Childhood Trauma and Recovery presents best practice in helping children affected by early life sexual abuse to recover and lead healthy lives. At its heart is the SACCS approach, pioneered by Mary Walsh, which was developed to provide such children with specialist care and treatment. By creating recovery teams that cross over traditional boundaries to put the child at the centre of all activity, the approach enables young people to replace unhealthy ways of thinking with stronger, more appropriate cause-effect mechanisms.

Drawing on decades of experience with thousands of young people, the authors challenge the view that simply placing traumatised young people in safe, loving environments will be sufficient for them to recover. They expose the challenges of caring for children who may be highly sexualised by abuse then show how, by ensuring that these children feel safe and trusted and learning to communicate with them effectively, practitioners can begin a process of actively helping them to heal.

The book is primarily aimed at practitioners in child protection and adjacent fields responsible for the 64,000 looked after children in the UK, as well as the millions more around the world. It will also be of interest to students and practitioners in fields such as social work, counselling, youth work, psychology and foster care.

Purchase your copy online at:
www.pavpub.com/childhood-trauma-and-recovery

£27.95 | 200pp | Paperback | 9781912755554 | Sept 2019